AMERICA'S
LEAST COMPETENT
CRIMINALS

OTHER BOOKS BY CHUCK SHEPHERD

News of the Weird

More News of the Weird

Beyond News of the Weird
(all written with John J. Kohut and Roland Sweet)

AMERICA'S
LEAST COMPETENT
CRIMINALS

True Tales of Would-be Outlaws Who Have Botched, Bungled, and Otherwise Haplessly but Hilariously Fumbled Their Crimes

CHUCK SHEPHERD

HarperPerennial

A Division of HarperCollinsPublishers

HarperCollins books may be purchased for educational, business, or sales promotional use. For information, please write: Special Markets Department, HarperCollins Publishers, Inc., 10 East 53rd Street, New York, NY 10022.

FIRST EDITION

Designed by George J. McKeon
Illustrations by Art Glazer

Library of Congress Cataloging-in-Publication Data
Shepherd, Chuck.
    America's least competent criminals : true tales of would-be outlaws who have botched, bungled, and otherwise haplessly but hilariously fumbled their crimes / by Chuck Shepherd. —1st ed.
        p.   cm.
    Includes bibliographical references.
    ISBN 0-06-095002-1 (pbk.)
    1. Criminals—United States—Anecdotes. 2. Crime—United States—Anecdotes. 3. Criminals—United States—Miscellanea. 4. Crime—United States—Miscellanea. I. Title
    HV6791.S44 1993
    364. 1'092'273—dc20   92-56271

93 94 95 96 97 ❖/RRD 10 9 8 7 6 5 4 3

CONTENTS

INTRODUCTION

The two premises of this book are:

1. Most criminals, fortunately, are not smart like you and me.

2. It is so far still politically okay to be unashamedly entertained by criminals' witlessness.

Let's get on with it.

Criminals' lack of intellectual ease is not a newly discovered phenomenon. In their landmark work, *The Criminal Personality*,[*] Samuel Yochelson and Stanton E. Samenow detail various studies of young delinquents, depicting them generally as possessing an "especially short attention span," less reliable, more careless, lazier, and more restless than their nonaberrant contemporaries. Furthermore, one researcher distinguished between ordinary inferiority complexes, which we "normal" people have from time to time, and criminals' "zero state," a qualitatively different experi-

---

[*]Samuel Yochelson and Stanton E. Samenow, *The Criminal Personality*. 2 vols. New York: Jason Aronson, 1976.

ence that drives criminals to take risks into the unknown, or the barely known, because of a desperate need for recognition.

Other studies cited by Yochelson and Samenow refer to the prevalence of "concrete thinking" (as opposed to "conceptual" thinking) among criminals. Concrete thinkers don't easily recognize the similarity between situations; they fail to learn by experience.

Yochelson and Samenow also cite studies judging criminals as perfectionists of sorts, at least as to those behaviors important to the criminal. When one or two things go wrong, errors tend to increase geometrically as these hapless miscreants fall back into the "zero state."

Those generalities describe criminals into the seventies, but few sociologists have had the opportunity to study the relatively recent drug-addicted criminals—those whose robberies and burglaries are "planned" not at all or at most in some very loose sense because of the sudden and uncontrollable need for money. Conceptual thinking by those guys is not even on the board.

If this criminal behavior is state of the art, it presents bad news and good news. The bad news is that more of our stereos are missing; the good news is that—though we all may have dark sides—we can reassure ourselves that we couldn't possibly have done things as stupid as the people chronicled in *America's Least Competent Criminals.*

All of these stories really happened. To me, and to the readers of "News of the Weird," that makes the stories more exciting than the perhaps even wilder stories that a fiction writer could manufacture. Fictional characters can be used as instruments to test human imagination, but the adventures in this book are benchmarks for the human experience.

Ground Rules

1. How do I really *know* that this stuff is true? I don't really *know*, but I've taken some steps to weed out the high-risk stories:

• No supermarket tabloids were used as sources. Actually, the stories in the *National Enquirer* and the *Star* are generally true, and even some of the stories in *Weekly World News* are true. But I can't risk using any of them because tabloid writers often exaggerate.

• No "secondary" sources were used. Each story comes from a mainstream daily newspaper or other highly reputable news source in which the reporter was assigned to find out the old who-what-when-where-why. "Columnists" or "feature" writers, whose job is to be entertaining, I figure might not have the same commitment to accuracy as a "reporter" has.

• I applied an "urban legend smell test" so as not to use any stories that might be one of those tales "that happened to a friend of mine" and thus are sworn to be true. Stories without enough proper names to check out, I discard. Those that look too good to be true, I make some phone calls.

Having said that, there's no doubt that reporters get stories wrong. Or the police exaggerate their adventures. Or witnesses lie. The stories in this book do present accurate reports of what witnesses told the police, and what the police told the press.

2. I don't generally follow up the stories, unless the news report I've seen is hopelessly incomplete. Consequently, I don't usually know what ultimately happens to these people. The vast majority, I'm sure, are convicted of something (they often plead guilty to lesser crimes). A few may ultimately not be convicted. Of the latter group, most will have been exonerated not because they are innocent, but because the government failed to prove guilt beyond a reasonable doubt. Theoretically, a few of the people described in this book may truly have been innocent—framed or the victim of police incompetence. Unless I specifically say that a person was "convicted," I am only reporting that he was "arrested" or "charged," and providing the allegations of witnesses that led police to arrest or charge him. The reader should not leap ahead to the conclusion that everyone I write about was "convicted."

Any peculiarities in the text not accounted for by the above explanation, of course, are the fault of . . . my editor, my parents, neighbors, teachers, and our national indifference to education.

3. I know of as many instances of incompetent criminals as anyone, but I can't pretend that my knowledge does more than scuff the surface of the "problem." Much of it is not reported—thought to be unworthy by the reporters or editors whose beat is crime. My own observation after practicing criminal defense law in Washington, D.C., is that if you dig deep enough into any crime, you find some stupidity. Unfortunately for the police, not all of the stupidity is as spectacular as the stupidity chronicled in *America's Least Competent Criminals*.

If you're a collector of these kinds of stories, drop me a line at P.O. Box 8306, St. Petersburg, FL 33738. We can exchange some classics. Or, if you're not a collector but just one day come across a story on the stupidest criminal you've ever heard about, please send me the clipping— especially if it's a story that happened in your town. Unless I get inundated, I'll write you back to thank you for helping me to extend this chronicle of the human experience.

Chuck Shepherd
St. Petersburg, Florida
April 1993

ACKNOWLEDGMENTS

I found a lot of these stories all by myself, but not enough for a very good book. The difference was supplied by loyal fans of "News of the Weird" who feel as compelled as I to share with the world any instances they encounter of inspired idiocy. These "News of the Weird" correspondents are characterized by a keen sensitivity to societal frailties, an indifference to good taste, and, alarmingly, possession of a sharp pair of scissors. (If you ever meet an actual, bona fide "News of the Weird" correspondent, uh, well, best smile a lot, make no quick movements, and always know the closest exit.)

With the publisher's grace, I attempt to do justice to those who have helped me. I beg anyone who feels unjustly omitted to forgive me, write me a note, let me apologize to you. (If you feel omitted and are tempted to engage someone to knock me off in retaliation, may I suggest Mr. Wesley Rankin in Chapter 7?)

The people whose treasures I mined most often were

Harry Farkas, Edward Kimball, John J. Kohut, Myra Linden, Chip Rogers, Jim Sweeney, and Roland Sweet.

However, even through only episodic bookkeeping, I know that the following people made great contributions to this book:

Ed Aderer, Jean Arnold, Jenny Beatty, David Bennett, Trapper Byrne, T. S. Child, Keith Clark, Stephanie Clipper, John Cook, Eddie Cress, Rick Davis, Dena Dickinson, George Duquesnel, Geoffrey Egan, Bob Eland, Paul Evans, Bob Fogelnest, Jonathan Ginsburg, Joe Goulden, Eugene Grealish, Annie Laurie Hardy, Arthur Healey, Carole Holien, Dave Hotaling, Elaine Howard, Chuck Jones, Paul Jones, Jim Kane, Ivan Katz, Wolf Kirchmeir, Jane Kochersperger, Robert Lacy, Steven Lauria, Everett Long, Dale Lowdermilk, Kathleen Mazure, Aurlie McCrea, Barbara McDonald, James McNally, David Menconi, Matt Mirapaul, Donald Mitchell, Ray Nelke, Pam Novotny, Claudia Ortiz, Jenny Parks, Matt Paust, Jacqueline Pincus, Yvonne Pover, David Ronin, Saul Rosenberg, Jay Russell, J. B. Smetana, Michael Smith, Marty Snyder, Debby Stirling, Tony Tellier, Lang Thompson, Francis Toldi, Elliot Trach, Elyse Verse, Denis Wade, Alan Wall, Pat Washburn, Debbie Weeter, Elaine Weiss, Tracy Westen, Sparky Whitcomb, Brian Wilson.

I would also like to thank some other maniacs who have been important to this venture, including Robin Andersen, Kenneth Anger, Patrick Bishop, Jennifer Burchett, Boyd Campbell, Michael Colpitts, Craig Cramer, Gaal Shepherd Crowl, Linda Cunningham, Ruth Czirr, Kurt Darr, Tim Dorr, Karl Engle, Annette Friedman, Sam Gaines, Michael Garrett, Catherine Gilbert, Leslie Goodman-Malamuth, Fritz Gritzner, Lurene Haines, Ted Hornbein, Dorothy John, Steve Johnson, Bob Jones, Herb Jue, Susan Kennedy,

Emory Kimbrough, Scott Langill, Harry Lewis, Mike Lewyn, Pete Lineberger, Les Loble, Bob Maslow, Wendy Middleton, Brian Minsker, Ken Nahigian, Tom Nelson, Phil Parker, Allen Pasternak, John Pell, John Peterson, Linda Phillips, Jerry Pohlen, Sam Randlett, Rollo Rayjaway, Claude Rinehardt, Joe Schwind, Lloyd Shand, C. C. Shepherd, Thomas Slone, Peter Smagorinsky, Milford Sprecher, H. Thompson, Marty Turnauer, Elizabeth Vantine, Bill Wheeler, Don Williams, Elliott Woodward, Bill Woodyard, William C. Young, and Susan Zurcher.

And a few more: Gary Abbott, Jim Alchediak, Linda Anderson, Tom Arnold, C. P. Baker, Suzi Baker, George Barnett, Ed Baumgarten, Michael Bergman, Bob Berky, Don Bloss, Randle Brashear, Dan Brennan, Peter Brooker, Dennis Brothers, Karyn Buxman, Terry Carter, Jesse Chan-Norris, Jon Choy, Roy Colegrove, John Connell, Thorns Craven, John Cunningham, Michael d'Amico, Henrietta Davis, Drew DeSilver, John Doucet, Peggy Duerr, George Duncan, David Durfee, Bill Ellis, Kevin Elm, Jamie Elvebak, Allen Estrin, Mike Farrell, Jim Ferguson, Joe Ferrandino, Fred Fox, Elizabeth Gallas, Marie Gerules, Glenn Greenwood, Barbara Gudenius, Jerry Hamm, Mr. and Mrs. "Ted" Henderson, Cindy Hildebrand, Steve Hill, Peter Hine, Bob Jakob, Frank Johnson, Craig Jones, George Joseph, C. J. Kilgore, Marty Klein, Chris Knisely, John Kopecky, Barbara Lawton, J. Michael Lenninger, Walter Maier, Tim Maloney, Mark Mason, Curt and Elizabeth Matlin, Anne McNeill, Carol Moore, Jim Mouritsen, Christopher Palermo, Rhobie Parker, Mary Parry, Edward O. Phillips, Neal Sager, Scott Sandbrink, Gretchen Sharpless, George Shevlin, Wes Simpson, Eric Smith, Cynthia Storm, Maurice Suhre, Maurine Taylor, A. Lee Thames, Martin Tropp, Will Ward, Marley Watkins, Matt Wehling,

Steve Whiting, and Thomas P. Wolf. I give special thanks to one of the all-time brilliant giants of American journalism, Jack Shafer, the editor of the *Washington City Paper*, who had the wisdom to give "News of the Weird" its first breath, and to Christine Van Lenten, who, laboring under the handicap of material saturated with poor taste, nonetheless produces excellent editing, on "News of the Weird" and on this manuscript.

1

"Hello, 911? I'm Wedged in This Bank Vault":

CLUMSY BURGLARS

First, in defense of hapless burglars, remember that most burglaries take place at *night*.

• It's dark. It's harder for the burglar to see what he's doing.

• It's usually quieter at night, so burglars have to be quiet, too. They can't use their normal range of motion.

• Property owners usually lock everything up at night. Therefore, the burglar first has to get into the place before he can take something out.

Also, remember that burglaries, like convenience store holdups, are crimes of choice for drug addicts, who are the least likely among all criminals to engage in strategic planning. Thus, the new night-tool technology (e.g., infrared goggles) is lost on most burglars.

Since most doors are locked at night, the question of how to get in seems paramount. Over the last five or six years, there has been a sharp increase in roof entries—through vents or chimneys. Besides the obvious advantages (minimal noise, no glass to deal with), I attribute the popularity to Bruce Willis's masterful ventwork in the *Die Hard* movies.

It seems as if almost every city now has its own failed vent burglar. Most are like Creston L. Nance, then twenty-seven, who was found dangling upside-down from a vent, entangled in the overhead lighting, one morning as employees of Best Products Company opened up in Clayton, Missouri. James Edward Burgess hung helplessly for several hours in a chimney in his doctor's office in St. Petersburg, Florida, until a secretary arrived at work in the morning and found him. He was still upside-down, waiting for rescue workers, while a police officer, looking up, read him his rights. John E. Sears, then twenty-one, got stuck in the chimney of a Warwick, Rhode Island, public library building one night. Oh, yes, and for some reason he wasn't wearing pants.

Several burglars have gone to that great vent in the sky. William James Oden, then twenty, tried to enter a Nashville Pancake Pantry through a vent, which, predictably, was slippery with grease. He slid down out of control, and his arm lodged tightly under his neck, strangling him. A similar fate befell Jeffrey Powell, then twenty-seven, in a Chinese restaurant in Chicago. It was January, and the body froze in the vent, not to be discovered until the next day when the chef noticed that smoke was backing up into the kitchen. (It turns out that Powell was a recidivist: He had just been released from the slammer for an earlier vent burglary of a liquor store in which his clumsy entrance triggered a burglar alarm.)

A burglar named Dennis Johnson, who was thirty-four, met his demise in a Memphis fast-food restaurant, where the vent, not surprisingly, is right above the french fryer, in which Johnson's feet dangled after he became stuck. The restaurant had just closed, and the oil was still quite hot. Though Johnson's cause of death was asphyxiation, the coroner said that Dennis's last minutes were not pleasant.

Battles of Wit with Panes of Glass

Burglar entries requiring the negotiation of *glass* are fraught with danger. How much noise will breaking glass make? Will the glass crack or shatter? Will it fall in or out? Will it nick the burglar's skin, or will it shred his body to pieces? Discovering the answers to these questions is a matter of trial and lots of errors.

Larry Shelton James broke into a First Union Bank building in Durham, North Carolina, by throwing a rock through a large window. However, he failed to realize that the bank's lobby was below ground, so that when he climbed through the window, it was a long drop to the floor. He fell onto the broken glass from the window and began to bleed badly. He was able to control the bleeding for a while as he rummaged through the bank. (HINT TO BURGLARS: Banks are not good targets for burglaries unless you need, say, a sofa or a plant. They lock up their money at night.) Finding nothing to take, and still bleeding badly, he turned his attention to leaving. The doors, of course, were locked. Since the bank floor was lower than the ground outside, the windows were all very high up and, for someone whose hands were badly cut, not reachable by climbing. Confronting the existential moment head-on, he finally, courageously, dialed 911 for medical attention, and was arrested.

Several others have been notably cut during the crime process. One found his way to a first-aid kit on the premises but left a bloody fingerprint that was his undoing. Another guy left his fingerprint at the scene—in the form of his actual finger, which was sliced off. Another bled to death during his getaway after slashing an artery.

Kenneth D. Huggins, then twenty-four, had two problems: First, the glass from the window he entered to burglarize the home of an eighty-five-year-old Nashville woman, and second, the eighty-five-year-old woman. She smashed him repeatedly over the head with a six-pack of canned Sprite. Allegedly, Huggins had begged the woman just to kill him because his cuts were so painful. A police officer said, after arresting Huggins, "He was cut worse than any human I've ever seen. [S]he wore his head out."

Once inside the premises, burglars' chief concern, seemingly, should be to avoid distractions. The police blotter is full of those who couldn't keep their eyes on the prize:

Kelly Lee Hardyman, then twenty, was caught red-handed in Gainesville, Florida, by the returning home-owner because he had become entranced with the owner's Nintendo setup. (It was his second burglary arrest in which he was discovered while playing Nintendo.)

Another fatal distraction is the telephone. Harold Schmidt, in Waukesha, Wisconsin, suspended the burglary process for a while to have a lengthy chat with his mother, long distance. Schmidt only became a suspect two months later—when the victim received her telephone bill, listing a call to Schmidt's mom. Mothers long for such thoughtful sons; she'll never deny that he called. Paul Caliguiri in Aspinwall, Pennsylvania, stopped to call his father. It was a local call, but Caliguiri somehow triggered the owners' answering machine, which recorded the touch tone sounds.

Violating the Cardinal Rule of Burglary

Mostly, burglars get into trouble stopping to eat, or drink, or take a nap, or watch some TV, or dress up in the missus's clothes. All of those activities are fun, but they violate the cardinal rule: Get the stuff and get out. The loser of all losers is no longer with us. He broke into a house in the Mission Hills area of Los Angeles one night in January 1989. He had lingered to have a nice meal and watch TV. And he had become a little sleepy. It would have been easy for him to see why he had become sleepy had he taken a good look, in the darkness, at the condition of the house he entered: It was covered by a large tent and many "FUMIGATION" signs. The next morning, neighbors found him "writhing" on the floor, but he failed to wake up.

In addition to the assorted behaviors of the Three Stooges School of Burglary—burglars shooting at each other, things like that—here are a couple of other examples of attention-deficit disorder:

A gang attempting to break into the Black Hawk Electrical Company in Cedar Falls, Iowa—a company known for the high quality of its burglar alarms—had to flee empty-handed after one of them tripped a burglar alarm.

And Cecelio Rodriguez and Armando Milian, trying to break through the steel doors of the Cash Mar Pawn Shop in Miami, Florida, with a power saw (and a portable generator to run it) were captured when police showed up, alerted by the burglar alarm. In fact, the alarm had been sounding for quite some time when the police arrived, but they found the two still industriously and earnestly attacking the door—making so much noise with the power saw and generator that they were oblivious first to the alarm and then to the cops standing right behind them.

2

"Hi, I'm Butch. I'll Be Your Robber Tonight":

CRIMINAL SELF-IDENTIFICATIONS

Given a choice, most criminals prefer anonymity during the crime process. However, effective law enforcement demands that we find out just who these guys are, and the sooner the better.

To identify criminals, relentless investigators sometimes have to employ sophisticated techniques of interrogation to coax recollections of the crime process from witnesses. But sometimes the criminal makes it easy for the witness to recollect.

It helps that, as criminologists believe, many criminals subconsciously seek notoriety. The two leading reasons seem to be (1) the need to be confronted with their shame and

(2) the desire to maximize a celebrity that they could not have gained in the lawful sector of society. But police officers, crime reporters, and judges have another explanation for why many criminals leave clues to their identities behind during the crime process: They are stupid.

"Bank Policy Prevents Our Handing Over the Loot Without Positive ID"

Take bank robbers, for example. Granted, bank robbery is complex and can tax the attention span. Much can go wrong. Robbers can drop things on the floor.

Thomas Malone dropped his wallet in the First National Bank in Syracuse, New York, while he was there making an unauthorized withdrawal. That made it quite easy for police to find him later.

People have left their jail-release documents behind, and their inmate ID cards. Gary R. Leonard, then thirty-four, was arrested for robbing the Key Bank in Syracuse after he left, on the counter, a completed car loan application for his wife.

Jack Pleasant lost his wallet during a burglary in Opelousas, Louisiana, but for some reason (NOTE TO READERS: Please be advised that the phrase "for some reason" shows up over and over in this book) he marched down to the police station to inquire if anyone had turned it in yet.

Peter Robert Arnoldi dropped his checkbook during a burglary at the Co-op Oil Association in Nicollet, Minnesota, and must have realized it soon after that. The arresting officer said, "I've got your checkbook.'" Arnoldi reportedly replied, "Yeah, I know. I'm fucked."

Yet More "Cardinal Rule" Violations

Robbers have been known to violate one of the fundamental holdup rules by failing either to write the holdup note on a *blank* piece of paper or to take the note back after the clerk has finished reading it.

Kevin Thompson, then twenty-six, was charged with knocking off the Midlantic National Bank in Bloomfield, New Jersey, in 1987. Kevin did not take back the holdup note, which was actually the back of his paycheck stub. (Kevin further embarrassed himself with his spelling; that's another reason to take the holdup note with you. "This is a stickup, keep clam [he meant "calm"]," and "no won will get hammed." Kevin, where's your pride?)

Terry Wilson, then thirty, wrote a too-cute note on the back of his probation/parole card, with his name neatly computer-printed. "Give me all your money," he commanded, "or else I'll shoot you. Bang!" The Sun Bank in Orlando, Florida, did not have to wait long to recover its money.

"Wow, Butch! That Disguise Is *Really You*, Man!"

Since robberies are face-to-face transactions, many crimino-Americans attempt to use some sort of a disguise. In the ideal world, a disguise hinders, rather than assists in, the identification process.

Eugene "Butch" Flenough, Jr., had a great mask for an Austin, Texas, convenience store holdup in 1989: his motorcycle helmet, with a Darth Vadar–like visor. One problem: Written on the front of the helmet were the words "Butch" and "Eugene Flenough, Jr."

In general, members of the crimino-American community would be well advised to monitor the kind of everyday identification they carry on their persons.

Barry Buchstaber, in San Mateo County, California, in 1989, was standing beside a car that had two freshly broken windows when a sheriff's deputy happened along. Buchstaber was, of course, "minding [his] own business" at the time, "taking in the redwoods." When the deputy asked for some ID, Buchstaber shrugged and said he wasn't carrying any. The deputy then insisted on *anything* that Buchstaber might have with his name on it. Well, just this piece of paper, maybe. It was a copy of a current arrest warrant for Buchstaber for driving with a suspended license.

A guy in Watertown, South Dakota, was arrested in 1992 as a result of an inattention to detail that has plagued quite a few criminals over the years. This guy went through a fast-food restaurant's drive-thru with his pants down to flash a female employee. But just a few minutes before, he had driven through for a food order and paid by personal check.

Teenage spray-painting vandals in Springfield, Illinois, had a short run in 1987. Lacking the street smarts of big city vandals who use pseudonyms, these three boys and two girls actually sprayed their *real* names onto Lincoln's tomb and other targets.

And finally, in Worcester, Massachusetts, police put out an APB in 1989 for a man charged with robbing a tailor shop.

According to the APB, the man had a 14 ½-inch neck, 18-inch shoulders, 39-inch chest, 35-inch waist, 25 ½-inch arms, and 41-inch hips. Police knew all that because minutes before robbing the tailor, the guy had been measured for a suit.

3

"Excuse Me—When's the Next Bus?":

THE ART OF
THE GETAWAY

In many crimes, the trickiest part is the getaway, for two reasons: First, only *some* of the circumstances can be controlled; traffic patterns, for example, may be unpredictable. Second, compared to an insular criminal act, the getaway presents a vastly expanded array of opportunities in which to screw up. The purpose of the getaway should be to exit the crime scene quickly with minimum chances for detection, so that the criminal can get home as soon as possible, jump into bed, and pull the covers up real tight. To assist the crimino-American, herewith is a list of:

Getaway "Do's"

1. Even if you are very stupid, you still have a better chance of success if you try to control your getaway than if

you allow others to control it. (For some, however, random chance may be an even more attractive alternative.) Therefore, *try to avoid making your getaway on a municipal bus*. We can appreciate the pro-environment use of mass transit, but jails have housed many civic-minded souls, such as Richard Stowell, then twenty-seven, charged with robbing the Chase Lincoln First Bank in Syracuse, New York, in 1991. (He was on parole for a 1988 bank robbery, from which he also tried to escape on a municipal bus.) There are many others, from Dallas, and Columbus, Ohio, and Hartford, Connecticut, for instance. A taxicab is only a slight improvement.

2. *Try to use a vehicle that can go really fast.* Jack Kelm of Greeley, Colorado, wanted in a string of robberies in 1989, is just one of several who have embarked on robbery careers using a bicycle as the getaway vehicle. Without exception, they have been *short* careers. (Kelm, by the way, was eighty-two years old at the time, and immediately upon his arrest demanded to be taken to the hospital, complaining of a urinary tract blockage. Yep—the old Urinary Tract Blockage Sympathy Ploy!)

Randall Marlow at one point had a fast vehicle—a motorcycle—but he gave it up for something less speedy. California highway patrolmen in Los Angeles chased his motorcycle—only because they wanted to ticket him for equipment deficiencies—but he continued to outrun them, weaving in and out of traffic on a freeway. Then, for some reason, Marlow pulled off into a neighborhood, abandoned the motorcycle near a golf course, and commandeered a golf cart. He was easily apprehended.

Marlow doesn't look that stupid next to the twenty-two-year-old man who tried to make his break in a five-foot-high wheeled arc-welder in Hutchinson, Kansas, in 1990. In addition to its being slow and fairly easy to spot, an arc-welder makes large, ugly marks in the street, so that even if the cops stop off for a half hour at the 7-Eleven, they can still pick up the chase. Raul Rosas Camargo was arrested at his home, which was easy to distinguish because it was the only one in the neighborhood with an arc-welder parked outside.

3. *Try not to be conspicuous.* Raul violated this one, too, as did James Richardson, then thirty-two, and Jeffrey Defalco, then eighteen, who tried to steal a three-ton safe in Canoga Park, California, in 1990. They dragged it home behind

their car, believing that it contained several thousand dollars. In fact, it was empty, but it still weighed three tons. Not only did the safe prevent the driver from going fast (see Rule Number 2), it scarred the pavement (see Arc-Welder Principle). It also made such a deafening noise, and the metal scraping on the rock of the pavement created such a shower of sparks, that people were drawn to it from blocks away. Said one witness, "It looked like they were towing a Roman candle." The two men said they had planned to break it open with a crowbar. (HINT: James and Jeffrey, the reason they're called "safes" is that you can't get into them with a crowbar.)

Douglas Eric "Dougie" Girard, then thirty-two, and his buddy were being chased by police in connection with the robbery of a children's clothing store in La Verne, California. They ducked into a nearby McDonald's and got in line, trying to blend in with the crowd. When police walked into the McDonald's, they saw thirty suburbanites waiting to buy their Big Macs, along with two heavily tattooed guys, both with money bulging out of their socks and one carrying a gun in his back waistband. (It wouldn't be easy for the police. Dougie took some hostages before surrendering six hours later.)

A corollary to Rule Number 3 is: *Try to avoid leaving a trail.* A thirty-four-year-old man was arrested in Seattle after robbing a Seafirst Bank on Sixth Avenue in 1991. Employees had watched him flee down the street and notified police that he had run into a TraveLodge motel. Police assembled massive manpower, SWAT teams and all, intending to conduct a room-by-room search. When they got to an inside hallway, however, they found a small trail of dollar bills that seemed to stop in front of one of the rooms, and inside they found their man.

4. *If you have a getaway vehicle, remember to take the keys.* Otherwise, in an urban area, someone might steal it while it's parked out front, as happened to William McNellis, then forty-three, while he was inside robbing a New Haven, Connecticut, bank in 1985. Or, as apparently has happened to other forgetful criminoids, they'll lock

the keys inside the getaway car, as Paul C. Benier, then twenty-three, did in Swansea, Massachusetts, as he was knocking off the Lafayette Cooperative Bank.

Two seventeen-year-old boys robbed a Seafirst Bank in Des Moines, Washington, a suburb of Seattle, in 1991. Their first mistake was not taking the car in for a full inspection the day before. As they emerged from the bank with money in hand, they discovered that the battery was dead. They got out to check underneath the hood, but the doors locked behind them, with the key still in the ignition and the loot in the front seat. They panicked and started to run away, but dashed smack into a police car responding to the call about the bank robbery.

5. If you're worried about all the details of the robbery, hire accomplices, but *try to find people whose IQ is at least in the "dull normal" range.*

Drivers below that IQ are less likely to think of basic considerations, such as whether the car has automatic or manual transmission, which is a crucial distinction for those who can't drive the latter. Below that IQ level, also, they might decide, as one fellow did, that while you're in the bank pulling off the heist, this sure would be a good time to get the car washed across the street; be back in just a minute.

After emerging from a burglary of a Dillard's department store at the Ward Parkway Shopping Center in 1991, a forty-one-year-old man in Kansas City, Missouri, must have wished he'd done a better job of screening his accomplice. As a security guard grabbed him in the parking lot, his less gifted partner jumped in the getaway car and started toward the grappling pair. Just as the car approached, the guard moved out of the way, and the car plowed into the other burglar, giving him a broken jaw, punctured lung, and several broken ribs.

6. *Bone up on local geography and traffic patterns.*

Rory Johnson made a really bad decision after knocking off The Liquor Station in Elkhart, Indiana. With a choice of two roads to exit by, he picked the wrong one. He had parked in back of the store to facilitate his getaway, but by the time he drove off, the road on that side of the building had developed a huge bottleneck because of construction; he was quickly sandwiched in by other gridlocked motorists. Five minutes after the robbery, as liquor-store employees emerged from the store, they spotted Johnson sitting in his car, which had moved only a few feet.

Stephen Le, then eighteen, and two companions didn't have a car, but they could have used a map. They were attempting a burglary in Larkspur, California, in 1989 when police broke in on them. Two ran off together, and when they passed a tall chain-link fence with barbed wire atop it, running parallel to the road, over they went because police were on their tails. The fence happened to be the outer perimeter of San Quentin Prison.

Sometimes it pays to take note of environmental conditions, too. In the brisk Kansas winter in 1989, two fifteen-year-old boys stole a car and tried to outrun the police. They failed, because the street had become almost a solid sheet of ice, limiting the boys' driving to about ten mph.

You should not route your getaway through a district that's packed with Secret Service and local police protecting the President of the United States while he gives a speech in the neighborhood, as Xavier Hunter tried during an appearance by George Bush, just after Hunter had robbed a Chicago bank. (Hunter was especially conspicuous on the street once the chemical dye pack exploded in the bank money he was carrying.)

These simple rules should take care of most getaway

lapses, but American criminals have reached high levels of creativity in mishandling the getaway.

Take Anthony Colella, then forty-nine, one of the best-known recent American bank robbers, thanks to what happened to him after he ran out of a Brooklyn savings bank in 1989 with $2,100. He had run about a block and a half down the sidewalk when another man leaped from a parked station wagon, slugged Colella, and took the money. Colella did what anyone would do under the circumstances: He walked down the street to the local police precinct and reported the robbery, whereupon he was arrested.

It may seem self-evident to some, but it bears remarking that the getaway is not the proper time for the driver to demonstrate his highway courtesy or knowledge of traffic rules. Two suspected burglars were chased away by police from Grif's Western Wear near Miami, Florida, at five o'clock one morning in 1989, and a high-speed chase wound through city and suburban streets and finally onto the Sawgrass Expressway. Police caught the burglars' car after the men dutifully stopped at the tollbooth to pay the fare. And in 1992 Philip S. Whaley, Sr., was captured and charged with grand larceny and other crimes in Syracuse, New York, after a twenty-eight-minute chase involving numerous route changes. For all twenty-eight minutes, Whaley signaled every single turn that he made. Said an officer, "We knew exactly where he was going."

Clichés Come to Life: The Role of the Bedsheet

Kourosh Bakhtiari, then twenty-seven, masterminded an escape from a New York City correctional center where he was temporarily housed on a weapons charge. He would lower himself out a window. Bedsheets, you assume. This jail was too sophisticated to provide them, for just that reason. However, most jails believe in dental hygiene, and packs of floss are abundant. Bakhtiari braided fifteen packs to make a rope, of sorts, to lower himself down, and what could be stronger than dental floss, anyway? However, he neglected to plan for anything like *gloves*: A 190-pound man lowering himself on dental floss puts quite a strain on his hands. He cut himself badly and severed various tendons.

William Sibila, then thirty-four, fell to his death in an aborted bedsheet escape from the prison ward at the Nassau County, New York, Medical Center in 1989. Dangling from the end of a twenty-foot-long bedsheet, which he had badly estimated would be enough to reach the ground, he found he was still thirty-five feet short of the cement landing. He leaped anyway, and fell on his head.

Futility as Art Form

Two men escaped in 1989 in Kansas City, Missouri, despite the failure of their unusual getaway plan. After robbing the Mercantile Bank, the two men threw out behind them boards they had prepared with nails protruding upward to puncture the tires of any pursuers. However, the first thing the men did when the boards were down was to run over one of them in their own car. Sure enough, it punctured a tire. They fled on foot.

Larry Quick, then twenty-five, thought it would be a good idea to rob a waterfront restaurant in Keego Harbor, Michigan, and to make his getaway by swimming across

24

Crescent Lake. The truth is that he was not that good a swimmer and had to be rescued by employees of the restaurant.

A seventeen-year-old burglar was captured in Red Wing, Minnesota, in 1990 and charged with stealing coins from an amusement park concession. He had jumped into the Mississippi River to escape pursuing police, but soon swam back to shore, exhausted. Police said he wasn't a good swimmer to begin with, and second, he was carrying too much extra weight, since his pockets were packed with coins from the burglary.

In 1991, two teenage boys being driven to juvenile court in Reading, Pennsylvania, by police officers managed to escape when the squad car stopped for a light. They eluded police for a while even though they were handcuffed together, but, running down a sidewalk, they failed to communicate with each other as to whether they would run to the left or to the right of the flagpole they were fast approaching. One went left, one went right, and they dazed each other as they collided on the other side. Nearby firefighters watching the incident took up the chase and caught up with the struggling kids.

Later that year, in San Francisco, Larry Schweinfurt, then thirty-one, had a similar catapult-type mishap. He had just threatened to rob a cab driver by brandishing a meat cleaver when the cabbie suddenly jumped from the slow-moving vehicle. As Schweinfurt tried to get out of the cab himself, the door banged against a parking meter and whipped back, striking Schweinfurt on the head and almost knocking him out.

4

"Officer, That Man Stole My Drugs!":

MAKING IT EASY FOR
THE COPS

Of all the stories that people never believe, the one they never
believe the most is about the fellow who marches down to
the precinct to report that his drug stash has been stolen
and to demand that the constables go get it back for him. It
happens. Why do they call it dope, indeed!

Gregory T. Mershad, then twenty-one, of Dayton, Ohio,
made his demand on the security guards at a Marco Island,
Florida, resort in 1983, saying that some-one had
stolen about $1,000 worth of coke from his room The.
guards actually recovered the stuff and called Mershad,
who looked it over and said, "It's mine, but a lot's missing."
The guards, and local sheriff's deputies, asked Mershad

to sign for the return. Said a guard, "I couldn't believe it when the goof signed the receipt." That was just what they needed to arrest him.

James Christopher and Tony Allen grabbed cops in El Paso, Texas, and demanded the arrest of the cab driver who gave them oregano when they thought they had purchased $50 worth of marijuana. And James Allen Manuel, then twenty-three, complained to Baltimore police that he was due a refund from a drug dealer—because what he needed *right then* was not cocaine but a prostitute. (Manuel apparently had no access to mirrors; his nose was ringed with cocaine residue at the time.)

Al Hamburg sued a woman in Torrington, Wyoming, for not honoring a fair-and-square contract. He claimed that he traded a car, valued at $300, to her in exchange for fifty "favors." What was the nature of the favors? the judge asked him. "Sex! S-e-x!" he shouted. If the woman had indeed made such a deal, evidently she came to believe she got the short end of it—although Hamburg claims she was two thirds of the way through her obligations when she threw in the towel. Hamburg likened the contract to a marriage agreement; the judge said it was prostitution. The lawsuit was thrown out, but Hamburg was not arrested.

"Officer, I'm Not Wanted for Anything, Am I?"

Imagine the delight of the Barberton, Ohio, police force when, one day in January 1991, Jack Carl McMorrow, then forty-seven, stopped by just to inquire whether there were any warrants outstanding for his arrest. Wait right here,

Mr. McMorrow, and we'll check. (Brief pause for computer search.) As a matter of fact, Mr. McMorrow, there are two. You're under arrest. You have the right to remain silent . . .

Kevin L. Jones, then twenty, went with his girlfriend to a police station in Richmond, Virginia, to post bail for a friend. While waiting for the paperwork to be processed, Jones and his girlfriend couldn't keep their eyes off a particular wanted poster. It was the wanted poster for Kevin L. Jones. As a police officer put it, "He looked up at the picture. His girlfriend looked up at the picture. Everyone else looked up at the picture. He got arrested."

Richard Brown is typical of another class of felons—the earnest citizen. The then-twenty-two-year-old ran up to a Boston police officer in 1982 to report that someone had thrown a firebomb into a nearby variety store. Several arson

episodes had occurred in the area recently, and police were edgy. One officer happened to look in Brown's car. He saw four gallons of gasoline and an actual firebomb and arrested Brown for the arson spree.

David Ferrell Marshall, then twenty-five, had worn distinctive pink and gray shorts in the robbery of a convenience store in Palatka, Florida. His getaway route took him by the nearby police station, and he decided for some reason to stop by and inquire about career opportunities in law enforcement. Marshall was ushered into Chief Dan Thies's office, and the two were chatting it up when Thies received a phone call about a robbery committed only a few minutes before by a guy wearing pink and gray shorts.

A man in Wichita Falls, Texas, who had come to the police station in 1989 to recover his impounded car was sent in to see the chief himself, Curtis Harrelson, because the man did not have enough ID to reassure officers that the car was his. The man courteously introduced himself to the chief by doffing his hat. Unfortunately, he had forgotten that that's where he kept his marijuana. Two packets fell to the floor right at the chief's feet. The chief was grateful; working at a desk, he doesn't get many arrest opportunities.

"That's Me—With the Explosives!": Photographing the Crime

The nineties: The Age of Celebrity. Enter the camcorder and America's funniest/screwiest/dullest home videos. A brand-new breed of idiots, who can't resist starring in their own productions, now hold up their stolen booty in front of the camera. They shoot tapes of themselves in the act of burgling, in the act of beating up victims. Those with technology anxiety rely on the staples of still photography and audiotape recording.

In Madison, Wisconsin, Dale Klitzke and Shawn Ambrose compiled a photographic record of their experiences vandalizing mailboxes with baseball bats. Conveniently, they had also left audiotapes with play-by-play commentary. Sample: "We are now leaving the apartment with the explosives. Matt's holding the recorder, and Dale's following faithfully behind him. So what's the target today? I figure a string of mailboxes should do." They also discussed at length their lack of fear of police.

Your English Teacher Was Right:
Spelling Counts

Crimino-Americans as a group did not have high grade-point averages. There are *no* recorded incidents where the failure to know algebra has resulted in arrest, but the jails are full of bad spellers.

It's easier for the cops to link two crimes if they can match the evidence. Washington, D.C., police knew they had the same guy when bank holdup notes kept turning up with the admonition to put the money in the bag "and no bullshirt."

Thomas Lee Jones, then twenty-four, was arrested in 1989 for robbing a Santa Barbara, California, restaurant. His holdup note had threatened "to shot" employees, so the police played a hunch. They set up roadblocks all around town. Officers asked each motorist who looked like the suspect to please step out of the car and spell "shoot." They got their man.

Arithmetic did in Lawry Adams, then twenty-seven, who had been charged with driving without a license in Harrison, New York. He had no identification when police stopped him, and he gave his brother's name. They asked him to spell the first name; he failed. They asked for his date of birth and Lawry gave a date, but when they asked the follow-up question ("How old are you?"), he didn't even come close.

They Always Return to the Scene of the Crime

It's not true that the only reason criminals return to the scene of the crime is to make sure they didn't leave any evidence. Mostly, they return to the scene of the crime because they're stupid.

Thomas Lancaster, then twenty-one, came back to the doughnut shop he had just robbed a few minutes earlier at knifepoint in Oxnard, California. He wandered in, sat down, and tried to order a cup of coffee. The clerk merely beckoned to the police officer who was taking down all the information for the robbery report, and he made the arrest.

It gets sillier. A successful bank robber who has just come into possession of a very large amount of money has also come into possession of a problem: asset management. Sensibly, he will want to protect his new nest egg from the ravages of risk and inflation, while getting the best return. Suppose he's risk-averse and rejects growth stocks, high-yield bonds, and commodities. Suppose he decides on a simple "time deposit" ("checking account" to you, who, unlike the robber, are not "in the business"). Some would criticize that choice as too conservative, but it is both convenient and safe—as long as the robber has not stolen more than $100,000, which is the maximum protected by federal insurance, an important consideration for protecting your money from, say, bank robbers. However, one would think it merely common sense that the robber open an account in a bank *other than the one he stole the money from in the first place,* unlike a guy in Champaign, Illinois, in 1985 or one in Portland, Maine, in 1986.

People who steal personal property usually want to fence the goods as quickly as possible. With such a sense of urgency, you basically work on the first potential consumer you see who possibly might be in the market for what you're offering. To some thieves, that means, inevitably, the person you stole the stuff from in the first place.

The case of Melvin Lewis Shelton is typical. Shelton, then thirty-seven, burglarized a car in Gainesville, Florida, in 1988, and then thought it would be a good idea to rais- money by selling the goods back to the owner. But the owner was busy at his office, and after several attempts, Shelton left a message—with his phone number. Said a police lieutenant of Shelton, a career criminal, "He's been in the system for twenty years. You'd think he would have learned some things by now."

Ricarles Wright, thirty-four, was accused by police in Waterloo, Iowa, of stealing two hams at gunpoint from a grocery store. Not a lot you can do with that much ham. Who would be more likely to buy the ham from you than that grocery store you stole it from? After all, they've now got a shortage, thanks to a recent robbery. That the hams still have the store label and date on them seems of minor importance. Wright was arrested when he returned, one hour after the robbery, to try to get a $45.58 cash refund.

The most perplexing cases of this genre are the dozens of cases of rapists who recontact their victims, not to harm them further, but to *date* them and propose marriage. Crazed for power and violent sex, they suddenly see the light. Their imaginations turn to white picket fences with rug rats running loose, PTA meetings, the Ozzie and Harriet family. At last, stability. The heart, as Woody Allen says, wants what it wants.

"My Momma Always Taught Me to Try to Be Helpful"

The thing about "habitual criminals" is what they're habituated to. If you've been "in the system" for a while, prison is your mama and your daddy and all you know. For a guy named Derick Grace, with three convictions under his belt by the age of twenty-two, his dependency on the Florida prison system was pretty severe. Within a month of his release from prison, police later said, he found time for two robberies. Cops happened along during the second robbery, and Grace was off, leading a high-speed chase from Palm Beach to Fort Lauderdale. He had apparently given the cops the slip and settled in for the night at Fero's Court Motel in the town of Dania. Motel registries, of course, ask a name, address, name of employer, things like that. Grace wrote down the only ID he knows— his real name, his prison ID number, and, in the space after "employer": "Department of Corrections." He was arrested shortly after check-in.

A twenty-four-year-old man just out of the slammer and looking at another ten years of parole decided to take a dip in a public swimming pool in Kenosha, Wisconsin, in 1988. He was packing a rod, which was a violation of his parole, and the locker room attendant at the pool said he'd have to check all of his clothing. Reluctant at first, but apparently longing for that dip, the man focused his apprehension by threatening to shoot the attendant if he told anyone about the gun. Not surprisingly, the attendant alerted authorities the second the man entered the pool.

Who knows what was going through the minds of Denise and Jeffrey Lagrimas of Oroville, California, when they volunteered to be the hosts of the latest "neighborhood watch" meeting in 1990. All the neighbors would be there, sipping refreshments in the Lagrimas' home while two police officers explained how residents could protect themselves from the latest rash of local burglaries. After the meeting was over, Nancy Miller waited outside for the officers and reported that not only had she seen her TV set and Christmas stockings in the Lagrimas' home, but that Mrs. Lagrimas was wearing Miller's dress. Armed with a search warrant, officers found $9,000 worth of stolen property.

Jesus Lezcano, then twenty, could hardly have been more helpful to Westminster, California, police officers in confirming his drunken status. They first encountered him standing beside his car, from which he had just emerged. The windshield contained a telephone callbox from the San Diego Freeway sticking through it, fresh from a collision over fifteen miles away. (Lezcano was not charged with driving while intoxicated because officers never saw him driving.) Lezcano averred that he did not know the callbox was there.

Three men in Salt Lake City appeared to be loitering near an underground parking garage when police officers asked them for ID. Each claimed to have none, but one was acting suspicious, and finally the officer persuaded him to clean out his pockets. One piece of paper was produced. It read, "If you don't want your family hurt, put all the money on the counter and spread out the bundles. Do it fast."

And police in Hallandale, Florida, were alerted by a Miami television station to charge Harry J. Bradley with murdering his wife. News reporter Art Carlson had received a call from Bradley announcing that he had killed her and then asking if the station would pay him for the information under its "news tip" policy.

5

"I Know This Sounds Crazy, But . . . ":

THE MODUS OPERANDI

We ordinary noncriminals—laypersons—associate the modus operandi (MO) with a feasibility study and a careful analysis of the costs and benefits of various options. However, for most crooks, the MO is the postperformance description of the series of improvisational decisions that constituted the crime. Crooks don't like to waste time in "advance" thought; they figure they will have plenty of time—years, perhaps—to think about the crime after they commit it. Even when they engage in such advance thought, the results are no better than if they acted upon whatever "default" settings their Creator gave them.

The MBA Mentality in the Criminal Industry
Notwithstanding our national expenditure of hundreds of millions of dollars on drug law enforcement, the invasion of

Panama, the temporary jailing of Pablo Escobar, and so on, large American cities still experience an *oversupply* of illegal drugs. That means competition, which leads inexorably to attempts at strategic marketing that might typically be recommended by Harvard Business School types. But the same marketing that gets customers to beat a path to your door will also let cops beat a path to your door. Examples:

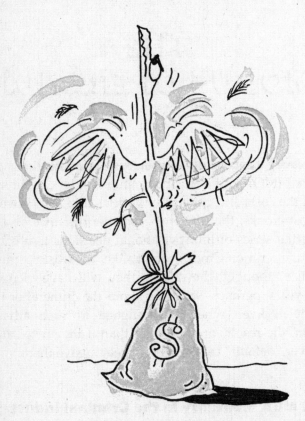

Marketing Premiums: Baltimore police shut down a drug operation offering giveaway coupons entitling the bearer to a $1 discount or to a free bag of marijuana with every five purchases. The coupon also gave the seller's address and announced "Tell Your Friends" and "Open 24 Hours." Police went to the address and made a deal through a small slot in the door before making arrests. Asked to describe the operation, one sergeant said, "stupid."

Advertising: More easy pickings for Baltimore police: A cop just happened by a street corner newspaper rack that held a sign announcing bags of marijuana for $10. He asked John E. Garrett, then nineteen, standing alongside, if the sign was his. "Sure. It's the only way I can get people to stop."

According to Indianapolis police, David C. Stelts and James P. Gates wanted only to advertise ordinary prostitution services ("services for any sexual needs") and conceived the idea of saturating the area with helium-filled balloons containing handbills touting the women available and listing the phone number. They sent up one (as a trial balloon, of course), but were distraught to learn the next day that it had come down in a police department compound. Officers called up, arranged a date, and arrested the two men.

The Importance of Clear Communication: So many questions, so little time: What kind of paper should be used for the holdup note? A nice linen finish, perhaps? Brown grocery bag? Perhaps a pad of slips with boxes to check off, requiring no editing or composition by the criminal (and thus no spelling errors!). If the criminal composes his own note, active voice or passive voice? Directly state the potential physical harm, or just allude to it?

Raymond Baker, then twenty-four, enjoyed a short, multiple-heist career in bank robbery in the Detroit area in

1982–83. A chronic problem, though, was his thoughtfulness in attempting to give the bank tellers not just the instructions (usually something like, "I've got a gun, put the money in the bag"), but some *perspective*. In his notes, Baker typically explained that he was sorry he had to do this but that certain misfortunes had befallen him and that he really is not a bad person, et cetera, et cetera. Said an FBI agent, sometimes it took "two or three minutes" for the teller to read the note and figure out what Baker wanted. By the time an earnest reader finished, of course, several robbery-prevention adjustments had been made by other bank personnel.

The C&W Pawnshop in Mount Gilead, North Carolina, was robbed in 1989 by a regular customer who apparently had nothing to hock just then but wanted cash anyway. He was also apparently inexperienced in the robbery game because the clerk reported to police that the man, noteless, uttered the stock holdup line, "I've got a gun," just as his hand was emerging from his pocket holding a knife.

New from Day-Runner:
The Criminal's Organizer

Not all crooks reject the idea of advance planning. A couple of times a year I hear of criminoids who have made at least rudimentary attempts at organizing their desks. After all, the typical criminal's pockets must be mad jumbles of paper: old holdup notes, bail bondsmen's business cards, lists of addresses of all-night convenience stores.

Haitian immigrant Guarionex Orasmy (technically, not yet a crimino-*American*) was caught attempting his getaway from a Sun Bank branch in Hollywood, Florida, in 1990. A search turned up a "things to do today" list, including:

> car
>
> money
>
> house
>
> clothes
>
> food
>
> to begin my new life.

Police later said Orasmy was the guy who, two days before the bank robbery, used a steak knife to convince a Ford dealer to give him a new car (and indeed, beside "car" on the list was a checkmark).

In a case that resembles a lower-intelligence version of the movie *Basic Instinct*, the it's-only-a-novel defense was raised by Robert Peter Russell. He was charged in Alexandria, Virginia, with the 1989 murder of his wife despite corpus delicti problems—namely, the lack of a corpse. The main piece of evidence was a computer diskette, found by a former co-worker in 1988 while cleaning out Russell's papers following Russell's discharge from the U.S. Marine Corps. In a diskette file labeled "MURDER" were entries such as the following:

How do I kill her?

What to do with the body?

Make it look as if she left

Plastic bags over feet

Rehearse . . . Mask?

Check in library of ways of murder—electrocution??

Wash tarp!! I may need to cut it?

At the time, the co-worker told Russell's wife, who was also a Marine captain, that she had better be careful. She failed to take the warning seriously enough. At trial, Russell said, oh, that was all part of a mystery novel he was writing.

Safecracking: Whatever Happened to Sandpapering Your Fingers?

Safes, like banks, are places where money and valuables are kept and thus appear to be good targets for crime. Unfortunately for the criminal, safes are usually kept locked, requiring some brainpower to figure out how to get the contents out. A quick way might be to knock the door off with some sort of explosive. It is frightening enough to imagine an ordinary, dull-normal criminal; what are we to think of a criminal who has explosives (or a blowtorch) and utterly no knowledge of elementary physics?

So many have failed. Robbers at a Midland, Texas, fast-food restaurant, or a gang of men dressed as ninjas operating around Concord, California, or robbers in Pittsburgh, or Pomona, California, or Salem, Massachusetts. Each had an occasional success; each at least once blew up or set fire to all the money in the safe.

Optimistic Shoplifters

That most shoplifters get away with their crimes only serves to highlight the really dumb decisions made by those who got caught.

Like Carlene Gray's MO. She thought she had a shot at walking out of Christopher Lin Ltd. in San Francisco in 1988 with a $30,000 full-length Russian sable coat, if she simply stuffed it between her legs under her dress and coat and just sort of waddled out. Just as squirrels seek acorns, security guards seek waddlers.

Give Carlene no more credit than Earleen Davis, then forty-seven, who was accused of waddling out of three Houston stores with a fox coat, a mink coat, and an 8" portable television set, respectively, between *her* legs.

And speaking of waddling, a guy named Thomas Waddell was arrested in Baltimore in 1989 when a police officer saw him, well, waddling down a street, minding his own business but resembling, in the officer's words, "the Michelin man." On closer inspection, the officer found that underneath Mr. Waddell's clothes were twenty-one live homing pigeons and a few dead ones. For some reason, they had been stolen from a neighboring breeder.

Selecting the Weapon: Gub? Nif? Bom? Chain Saw?

As you'd expect, the choice of weapons for a robbery is dictated more by availability than usefulness. The amateur criminologist will detect that it is far more important simply to *have* a weapon than it is to have an effective weapon.

Karen Lee Joachimi, then twenty, of Lake City, Florida, was arrested and charged with attempted robbery of a Howard Johnson's motel late at night. She walked into the office and made menacing threats toward the clerk with a chain saw she had picked up on the property. No, she had not started it up, and no, she probably didn't even know how. The clerk's brother knocked it out of Joachimi's hands to foil the robbery.

Lloyd Walter Dickerson, then thirty-six, tried to rob a Maryland National Bank branch in Baltimore, armed with at least two homemade bombs. Inside the bank, he first wanted to establish his credibility as a menace. He handed over a note that said the teller had exactly "three seconds" to give up all the money or a bomb would go off. The teller scrambled, but getting that much money together by "one-Mississippi, two-Mississippi, three-Mississippi" is no small task. So Dickerson set off the first bomb, which merely filled the room with smoke. "Well, anyway...," he might have said, "you get the idea. Now, give me the money." After he had the money, he gratuitously set off the second bomb, which actually shattered some windows and blew out the wall into which the ATM was installed. By this time, the employees and customers were so ticked off at Dickerson for all the smoke and inconvenience that they chased him down the street, aided by passing police officers who had seen smoke billowing from the bank's now-shattered windows and who saw the man toss away his wig and attempt to unbutton a long overcoat while fleeing the angry mob. Despite the two explosions, the only injury was to Dickerson's hands.

Michael Smith, then twenty-nine, was arrested in Rochester, New York, in 1990 for a street-corner robbery of a couple getting out of their car. His weapon of choice was a realistic toy gun. However, the female of the couple reached into her glove compartment and pulled out her own realistic toy gun, leading Smith to drop his realistic toy gun and plead for mercy. As Smith started to run away, the couple screamed, alerting a neighbor, who chased Smith a short way and leveled him with a baseball bat to his insubstantial cranium, drawing blood. Smith escaped, but police followed the trail of blood and soon apprehended him.

Disguise Management

If even the best-laid plans for foolproof disguises can wind up short, think of where the worst-laid plans wind up.

A man robbed an Exxon station in Clayton County, Georgia, while holding his mask (of a large animal) in his hand the entire time. Not surprisingly, he was later identified as the robber by the station attendant.

Mr. J. Douglas Creswell pulled off at least three robberies in 1987 (for which he received twenty-five years in the Big House after a trial in De Ridder, Louisiana). The first two (of the same clothing store) were modestly successful, but the third did him in because his getaway was critically delayed. Problem: He had worn a large plastic garbage bag over his head as a disguise as he entered the Park Motel, but had not remembered to cut eye holes in it. Realizing his error too late, and apparently not being good at thinking on his feet, he wavered on the choice of whether to remove the bag to see where he was going and or just to continue to flail away (while trying futilely to pinch eyeholes in the bag with his fingers) as he struggled toward the door. He was delayed sufficiently that the police nabbed him shortly after he left.

More Improvisational Strategic Planning

Phillip Shane Duncan, then eighteen, didn't really have a handle on his MO when he put his hand inside his shirt (no weapon, though) and entered the Jet Market in Knoxville, Tennessee, in 1989, demanding money. The Jet Market is one of those places in which the clerk (at least at 4:32 A.M., which was the time of the robbery attempt) sits inside a bulletproof cage. Duncan could not understand why no money was forthcoming through the little drawer, and became hysterical. He and three cohorts began hollering and trashing the place, but still got no money. However, the loud noises did attract a passing police officer, and the four were arrested on the premises. Duncan had thought to wear a disguise, though. Over his head was an empty twelve-pack of beer, and he peered through the little handle holes as he conversed with the clerk.

Robbers' problems with the bulletproof cage were allegedly addressed by a man trying to knock over a gas station in Ionia, Michigan. It sounds urban-legendy, but here it is. The clerk in the booth wasn't budging. Okay, said the robber, either open that door or, or, or . . . I'll call the police. Unlike some variations I've heard, the guy in Ionia actually called 'em, and they came and arrested him.

Surprisingly, burglars more than once have been done in because, before the job, they had been assigned baby-sitting duties that they apparently could not get out of. Newark, New Jersey, police eventually found the man who had taken jewelry and $600 from a woman's home in 1991. Accompanying him was his four-year-old daughter, whom he left behind at the scene. The victim, who hid in a bathroom during the burglary, said she heard the little girl talking all during the burglary, saying, "Daddy, I'm hungry," and "Daddy, I have to go to the bathroom."

Okay, okay, *one Canadian* in a book of America's Least Competent. Jack Santos, then twenty-nine, demonstrated what police and reporters called elaborate planning for a Toronto bank robbery in 1992, including a hair-color disguise. Santos decided to bleach his dark hair the night before the robbery. However, when he woke up the next morning, his hair was not blond but bright orange. He decided to go through with the job anyway, which involved dressing in a business suit, parking his car in the basement parking garage of the bank building, using phony ID to get to the bank president, threatening bombs in the building, and taking a taxi and escaping with $3 million. However, when he got home from the robbery, he realized his apartment keys were still inside his parked car, and when he went back to the bank building to retrieve them, cops had no difficulty spotting the guy with orange hair.

6

"Trust Me":

DREAMS
AND SCHEMES

For the first time in half a century, American ingenuity is being questioned worldwide. The country that invented almost everything worth inventing now seems to be awaiting the next breakthrough from Japan. Have we become too fat, too smug to develop and produce? Is American creativity what it used to be? If activity in the criminal sector of our economy is any index, I submit that our national imagination is as fine as it has ever been. I submit as proof these stories—some of the finest contemporary harebrained schemes anyone has ever, even momentarily, thought he could get away with.

For instance, stealing *wire*. Wire apparently became a preferred target for theft in the early eighties as the prices of certain precious metals rose and the secondary market, among carpentry and electrician supply houses, expanded. Usually thieves stole it from manufacturers' warehouses or hijacked shipments in transit. The less sophisticated thieves stole copper wire from utility poles—as in "live" electric lines. Some of those thieves went to jail, still nursing severe burns (like the guy who tried to victimize Georgia Power Company in Cartersville, Georgia, in 1989). On the other hand, some of them are dead.

Following the report of a theft of any kind, the first question that usually occurs to the police, the press, and the public is, "Who did it?" In an increasing number of cases, however, the question now being asked is, "*Why* would he do it?"

For example, in Glendale, California, in 1990, Thomas Joseph Bowman, then forty-six, a repairman for the city, was arrested and charged with stealing about nine tons of bricks from construction sites, hauling them away, and burying them in his backyard. Police found 1,327 bricks interred in a 20-foot-by-30-foot hole behind his house. It took workers fourteen hours, using a forklift, to dig them all up. Presumably it took Bowman himself even longer to put them there, even though the market value of everything in the ground was less than $3,000. Said Bowman at the time of his arrest, "I'm in bigger trouble than I realized." If Bowman thought this was a worthwhile use of his time, he certainly is in bigger trouble than he realized.

The same is true for two men arrested in Clayton, Missouri, in 1990 for stealing gutters and drainspouts from several homes and then selling them as scrap metal. The relatively high list price of the metal was the drawing point. However, since it took the men several hours per home to dismantle the pipes and gutters, and more time to carry them away and to arrange for a buyer, and since scrap metal goes for a lower price than unused metal, the police figured the men were actually clearing about $8 per house.

Two men attempting a burglary of a meat warehouse in Denver, Colorado, in 1976 made one of the more embarrassing misjudgments in the annals of American crime. Police officers discovered them outside the warehouse loading boxes of frozen meat into their car, ready to drive

off and presumably to resell the meat to supermarkets or consumers. As the men were being driven to jail in a police car, two officers began to joke about the crime, allowing the burglars to overhear them. It turns out that the burglars had inadvertently taken a shipment of "ren-nets"—inedible rectal tissue of cows—which is sold only to dairies to cure cheese. The officers began to laugh, whereupon one of the burglars in the backseat uttered this statement: "If I go to jail for stealing twelve hun-dred beef assholes, I'm really going to be mad." The men pleaded not guilty, and at their trial, the police officers testified as to that statement, which is, of course, part of the "anything you say" that "can and will be used against you in a court of law." Filbert G. Maestas appealed his conviction on the grounds that the state-ment was tricked out of him by the officers' laughter, but a state court of appeals laid the matter to rest the following year.

In 1991 Lyle Craig Bain, then a city alderman in New London, Wisconsin, was convicted of a gigolo-type offense. Bain had printed a sales brochure featuring his far-from-studly body as the choice product, offering "treat-ments" for women. The price list covered services ranging from dating to fondling to intercourse (which went for $65). Bain's offerings of course came with a money-back guarantee, and blank sales contract forms were also found. The services he performed, related the brochure, "were things most women only dream about." He had hired two women to help him promote his services, but one of them was an undercover cop.

Carnell Wilder, then twenty-five, wanted desperately to be a police officer in Philadelphia, but feared failing his written exam. He employed his girlfriend to imper-sonate him on the exam because he thought she was smarter and had a better chance of passing. But instead of just letting her take the exam and see what happened, Wilder for some reason thought *both* of them should take it, each using Wilder's name. Authorities were tipped off when Wilder both passed the exam (i.e., her paper) and failed it (i.e., his). Wilder is now in another line of work.

He wasn't as dumb as Ronald Sturkes, a twenty-seven-year-old white man, who made a nuisance of himself in the Hicksville, New York, driver's license office by complaining about the driving portion of his test. Then, to improve his chances of passing the written portion, he sent an impersonator. However, since everyone knew him in the office, it is not clear why he thought sending a fifty-five-year-old *black* man was a good idea.

In 1984, Gregory Thomas Filardi, then thirty-five, manager of a White Plains, New York, subsidiary of a large brokerage house, intercepted a $51,000 check his company had made out to the Mellon Bank, of Pittsburgh, then one of the largest in the United States. He took that check to a local bank and opened an account for "Mellon Bank." A few days later, he returned to the bank and attempted to withdraw $3,850, telling the bank employee his name was "Mellon E. Bank." A clerk called the FBI, and agents burst through the door while Filardi was still talking.

"Ahh, Nothing Like the Open Road, the Wind in Your Face, and the Acceleration of a Steamroller"

Psychologists tell us that some people experience a need from time to time, when encountering a vehicle, just to get in and drive it away. They may bring it back soon enough, and undamaged, but at the point of first seeing it, it becomes an object that simply must be experienced. Perhaps joyriders believe they won't be caught, or that they will and it's worth it, or that nothing else matters right then, anyway.

The vehicles themselves run the gamut. Cars, especially sports cars, are logical targets, but what about buses, cranes, garbage trucks, forklifts, backhoes, and various construction vehicles? Richard Booker Branch, then eighteen, stole a fifteen-ton cement mixer near Bartow, Florida, and stayed ahead of slow-moving police for an hour, through eight towns, before they shot his tires out. Michael S. Doughty, then twenty-four, broke into a warehouse in Portland, Maine, and stole a forklift, which he simply drove back and forth in front of the place until police made him get off. In 1988 a Los Angeles man, who later said only that he had been "tired of walking," stole a steamroller and tried to drive it away. Police eventually arrived and began a harrowing five mph chase, until one officer jumped aboard and subdued the man.

"Well, Where Else Am I Going to Come Up With That Kind of Money?"

Some crimes look inexplicable at first glance, but on closer inspection, an internal logic emerges. Danny Heitman needed $550—the fee for the $5,500 that AAA Bail Bonds in Tucson, Arizona, had just paid to spring him pending his trial for three counts of holding up branches of the First Interstate Bank. Heitman asked bondsman Frederico Luna to drive him "to the bank" to get it. While Luna's associate waited outside in the car, Luna and Heitman went into the bank, and Heitman filled out a slip and walked to the teller's window. At this point, Luna started to walk back to the car to prepare to leave, but a few seconds later, he saw Heitman running from the bank, clutching a fistful of cash, followed a few seconds later by the teller, yelling, "I've just been robbed."

Thinking Small, Thinking Big

I don't siphon much gasoline myself, so I can't decide whether it's really stupid or just moderately stupid. (I also can't decide whether this really happened or not; it's one of the few items in the book that do not really fit the criteria I've set out in the Introduction.) A teenage boy in Seattle in 1991 apparently decided to siphon gasoline from a recreational vehicle. Officer Tom Umporowicz got a call from owner Dennis Quigly that there was a boy lying on the ground outside the RV, and that he had been vomiting. Quigly's best guess is that the boy mistook the sewage tank for the gasoline tank.

As the reader has seen from stories in this chapter, criminals often lack a sense of proportion in the crimes they commit. They take extraordinary risks for ordinary rewards.

However, not Robert Haag, then thirty-three, of Tucson, Arizona. He was detained briefly in Argentina in 1989 on charges that he conspired to arrange to steal one of the world's four largest meteorites, a thirty-seven-ton one, the size of a large car, and smuggle it out of Chaco province. "This has been a super adventure," he told a reporter. "[A]ll kinds of [people] were trying to sell me meteorites." (HINT: Robert, customs officers can find drugs in false AAA-size batteries in transistor radios; what made you think you could smuggle out a meteorite?)

My favorite story of big-time thinking, from an undated UPI clipping from the seventies, identifies unemployed insurance salesman James William Cosgrove as the "brains" behind a scheme in St. Louis to bilk a local businessman out of money to fund a phony scheme to steal a submarine. Cosgrove told the man, "Getting a nuclear submarine is not as difficult as it's made out to be." Cosgrove and an associate said they planned to hijack a sub as it moved out to sea from New London, Connecticut, and deliver it to the Mafia. The asking price was $150 million "in small bills." Cosgrove also offered an "optional bonus," if the Mafia were interested, of dropping a bomb on Washington, D.C., during the President's State of the Union address. The businessman, of course, didn't believe a word of this and called in the FBI.

Money That's Not Worth the Paper
It's Xeroxed On

Arguably the most difficult, intricate crime may be counterfeiting money. Wait, let me rephrase that. The most difficult, intricate crime may be *successful* counterfeiting. Unsuccessful counterfeiters are everywhere, particularly in jail, having failed to live up to their career expectations. Color copiers are a major culprit now; they produce money that looks just fine to the incompetent counterfeiter but is not nearly good enough to fool people who work around money all day long.

The most inexplicable counterfeiting caper on record, I am quite confident, was pulled by James E. Sanders of Baton Rouge, Louisiana, who was convicted of trying to pass a single bogus $20 bill. His sentencing judge, U.S. District Judge John Parker, said this was "the most inept counterfeiter I ever heard of." He had cut the corners off a $20 bill and pasted them over the ones on a one-dollar bill. His decision not to produce in volume was his soundest one.

Several potential counterfeiters have been intercepted in

the production stage. Think about it: It's difficult to buy the supplies needed for a good counterfeiting job.

Michael Stohr, then twenty-six, was arrested in a printing-supply store in Madison, Wisconsin, after alert employees notified the police of a suspicious customer. Stohr had lingered for a long time beside a color chart, holding dollar bills up to it until he was sure which shade of green ink to order. After he placed the order and left, store employees copied down his car's license plate number.

Joseph T. Hill was convicted in 1990 in Orlando, Florida—officially the first U.S. citizen ever convicted of counterfeiting *Polish* currency. Among his work, done on a Canon color copier, were three million zlotys, which the court valued at $316. The federal agent who arrested Hill told reporters, "He could have printed a boxcar full of them and not have enough to buy an expensive suit."

By the way, if any reader *has* some bad counterfeit bills to pass, may I suggest heading for Fort Smith, Arkansas, and trying to pass them at Food 4 Less, Big Little Mart, and Yeager True Value Hardware—if, indeed, those stores are still in business. Those are the places that accepted crude, photocopied $100 bills from two men in January 1989.

7

"Don't Give up Your Day Job":

MORE BAD CAREER CHOICES

Kenneth Lang, then thirty-two, was arrested for knocking off a 7-Eleven in Old Orchard Beach, Maine. The clerk had seen Lang outside, struggling to put some black nylon on his head. As soon as Lang came through the door, he realized that he couldn't see past the nylon. After a few seconds of struggling, he simply took it off. His second problem was that he was armed only with a small paring knife. Said the clerk, "If he's going to make a career of this, somebody should tell him to at least get a real weapon." Lang stuck the knife in the clerk's side, then told him to lie on the floor while Lang went through the cash register. Soon Lang realized he couldn't get the drawer open and ordered the clerk to get back up and help him. Then he took the money and coins and stuffed them into a paper bag, which soon broke, sending coins rolling all over the floor. He ordered the clerk to get down on his knees and join him in picking up all those nickels and dimes. He then told the clerk to open the safe. Most people who have been to convenience stores lately know that safes are time-operated and that clerks can't open them, but that didn't stop Lang; he jabbed the paring knife harder into the clerk's ribs, hoping *that* would convince him. When the clerk said that hurt, Lang backed off. During this time, customers were coming into the store and up to the register to pay for things. The clerk said he couldn't wait on them because he couldn't make change; Lang had all of it in his bag. So Lang began helping the clerk make change for each customer by fishing through the coins. Police arrived just as Lang was leaving and a high-speed chase ensued, but Lang soon abandoned his car and was subdued by police officers and a police dog.

On a Wednesday morning in June 1991, a man in his late twenties or early thirties rushed toward a convenience store in Cape Girardeau, Missouri. A scarf obscured his face, and he carried a semiautomatic handgun. The clerk, who was cleaning up inside, saw him try hard several times to push open the door before he finally withdrew in frustration and left. As a police officer later explained to reporters, "The problem was that in order to get the door open, you have to pull, but he was pushing." There was indeed a sign on the door indicating that the door should be pulled.

Just Say "No" to Armed Robbery

Several potential criminoids have gotten all dressed up for a crime only to suffer the ignominious fate of having no one take them seriously.

A teenager in Mount Vernon, Washington, dressed in green fatigue pants and a baseball cap and wearing a bandanna over his face, had visions of the perfect robbery of the Edgewater Tavern one Thursday evening. Packing a rod, he walked in and announced a holdup. However, his voice was pretty high for a robber, and his nerves were acting up. Despite the gun, a couple of the customers started to giggle, then others followed suit, and pretty soon everyone was turned back around doing what they had been doing before the boy came in. The boy put his crime career on hold and dashed out the door.

Philadelphia police reported that on February 22, 1984, a man tried to rob four banks and a check-cashing agency, all within a five-block area, within a twenty-minute span, and was turned down each time. In three of the cases, he was turned down flatly by the clerk, but in two the clerks had panic attacks, frightening the man and causing him to flee.

Michigan state police in Ypsilanti reported in 1990 that a man had come into a Burger King at 7:10 in the morning, flashed the handle of a pistol, and demanded cash. The clerk informed the robber that he could not open the cash drawer unless the robber bought something. The robber thought for a few seconds, then demanded onion rings. As everyone knows, onion rings are not available until lunch time, and the clerk said so. Apparently frustrated, the robber walked out. Carl Bullis, then thirty-one, fell apart as well when informed by a teller at a Manufacturers Hanover bank in Buffalo, New York, that she could only hand over money to him if he had an account at the bank. Bullis did the only thing a man could do under the circumstances: He took his business to another bank. Across the street, at a Citibank branch, they were more understanding, but he was apprehended a short time later.

Alan Oser of New York says he was mugged in the seventies, and although I don't have a bona fide news story on it, his report comes from the "Metropolitan Diary" column of the *New York Times*, so ... As he was passing a vacant lot late at night, Oser, a journalist, had on his mind a couple of his friends' mugging stories, and just at that instant, a mugger popped up. "The coincidence was too amazing to be believed," Oser later told a reporter.

"I burst out laughing." The bewildered, but knife-wielding, robber demanded Oser's wallet. As Oser later reconstructed the conversation, he then said, "You can have my wallet, but first I've got to tell you a funny story [meaning the coincidence of his thinking of his friends' muggings]." Said the robber, "Don't want to hear no funny story." Said Oser, "No, no, it'll only take a minute." "Let's have the wallet." "No, no, just a minute." After a few more exchanges, and aware now of a crowd of people moving toward them, the mugger said, "Ahh, forget it," and walked away.

The Failed Hit Man: "It Wasn't *My* Fault—Guy Wouldn't Hold Still"

Wesley Rankin, then forty-four, consistently failed to pull off his duties as a hit man—in a feat that rivals the plot of the Kevin Kline–Tracey Ullman movie *I Love You to Death*. It started in Philadelphia, when Alfons Kesseler wanted to rekindle a romance he had had with a woman named Cathy, who by then was married to Edward Coulter. He hired Rankin to eliminate the husband. First, Rankin tried but failed to run Coulter's car off the road with a truck. Three months later, he shot an arrow at Coulter but missed. Then he threw a Molotov cocktail through Coulter's window, but it failed to ignite. Two months later he was all set to put a pipe bomb into Coulter's car, but it exploded while Rankin was in Coulter's driveway, tearing off Rankin's right hand and maiming his left. Rankin was paid $2,700 for the hit.

With Stella Valenza, then twenty-three, of New York City, it wasn't as much the incompetence of the hit men she hired as her own. She paid three teenagers a $1,000 down payment (with $19,000 to come) to knock off her husband. When their baseball-bat beating of the man failed to kill him, she agreed to pay them $150,000 to do the job right. Mr. Valenza then took six gunshots from the youths, but survived, prompting Stella to raise the ante to $300,000 before the cops tracked her down.

Joseph Randle, Jr., then forty-four, worked alone on his suicide. Distraught after murdering his girlfriend in Houston, Randle attempted to check out using the following approaches: He slashed his wrist, but stopped after a small cut because he said it hurt too much. He set out to drown himself but stopped because the water was too cold. Hoping to get lung cancer, he speed-smoked two packs of cigarettes. Hoping to be poisoned, he forced down a package of rancid chicken. Finally, feeling even more a failure than ever before, he turned himself in to police.

Criminals on the Left Tail of the Bell Curve

Richard Herdon was arrested in New York City after a string of bank robberies in 1988. Police say he tried twenty-five jobs over a forty-four-day period but that only on seven occasions could he convince tellers to hand over money, and that the seven only netted him $12,000 total. Said one officer, "He just didn't come across stern enough." The officer said Herdon was "the least successful bank robber we've ever had."

A Wilmington, Delaware, courtroom was the scene of an inept job of contriving testimony in 1990. Prosecutors had charged Roy H. Cantler with robbing the Wilmington Trust Company's Barley Mill Plaza branch, but it was Earl F. Laughton who confessed. At first, prosecutors accepted the admission, but there was something about it that bothered them, and they decided to keep the case against Cantler open a little while longer. At trial, Laughton was preparing to take the stand and tell the fabricated story when a prosecutor moved a briefcase and jarred papers from Laughton's hand. Laughton could not find the "cheat sheets" that Cantler had prepared for him to testify from. Laughton tried to fake the answers and got virtually every piece of information wrong, sending the courtroom into a buzz. Finally, Cantler could stand it no more; he threw up his arms and declared, "Hey, the party's over." Cantler, a career criminal, would have received a much harsher penalty than would Laughton for the crime, and Cantler had convinced Laughton to take the rap.

On November 23, 1988, a man about 6'3" and 160 pounds tried to rob the same branch of the First Virginia Bank in Arlington, Virginia, twice within a four-hour period. The first time, the teller placed the money in a bag, along with a red dye pack that would later explode and coat the money with a chemical. The man made it only a short distance out the door before the explosion, which scared him and caused him to flee, leaving the money on the sidewalk. The second time, the teller did the same thing; the man made it just as far as he did the first time before the dye pack exploded and he again ran off, scared, leaving the money on the ground.

Fifteen years after the fact in Staffordville, New Jersey, they still talk about Glen Niewiarowski and the Ricardo brothers and one jewelry store burglary too many. Their MO was to tie themselves to one long rope, break in through the roof, lower one of the men down to take the jewels, and lift him out. The owner of the store that became the gang's last stop was wary of the recent burglary spree and put a sign on the safe, "DO NOT TOUCH SAFE—IT WILL EXPLODE," which scared Glen as his colleagues lowered him down. Glen yelled up for instructions; the Ricardos told him to ignore the sign. Glen started to work but was startled by the electronic-eye camera in the room. It had nothing to do with the safe, but Glen had had enough. He yelled up that he must have tripped the explosives. The Ricardos did what any two reasonable people would have done under the circumstances: They ran and jumped off the roof, which meant that Glen, attached to them by rope, was catapulted up through the small hole in the roof, which then became a much larger hole in the roof. Glen, also in a hurry to get off the roof, jumped, fracturing his heels, and a police search of area hospitals that night turned him up.

But Dale Duff may have preyed on a judge's pessimism about the state of American criminal competence. Duff, a Texas parolee, was charged with burglary in Huntsville in 1987 but was found not guilty. When the prosecutor introduced evidence about Duff's criminal past, Duff's lawyer called Duff to the stand to testify as sort of an expert witness on crime. Duff's lawyer asked questions like, "Would an experienced criminal have banged on the door so long when he heard a TV set going inside?" because that's what happened in the case in which Duff was charged. Eventually, so many stupid acts were attributed to the burglar in this case that the judge acquitted Duff as too professional to have committed the crime.

Hopeful Signs: The Saga of Tracy Jay Jones

America needs more people who just will not take "no" for an answer. In March 1990, Tracy Jay Jones sought to improve his financial status by robbing the A&J adult bookstore in Dallas. He walked in and pulled off the robbery. As a former employee of the bookstore, he knew also that there was a handgun behind the counter, so he demanded that, too. However, as he was trying to stick this new acquisition into his waistband, he shot himself in the genital area. Obviously in great discomfort, Jones managed to stagger away, but without the money for which he had just given so much of himself. The very next night, to the great surprise of the bookstore clerk, who should appear but a badly hobbling Tracy Jay Jones, on crutches, holding with one hand the heavily-bandaged area bulging through his clothes and with the other his untrustworthy gun, and this time making off with the money. (So what if he got caught? He was sentenced to forty years after reportedly rejecting a plea bargain of twenty-five years, but the important thing is that American perseverence is *back!*)

8

"Officer, I Said I've Got Rugs, Man, Not Drugs!":

ATTENTION-SPAN FAILURES

The burglar at the First Church of Christ in Danville, Indiana, made off with a computer in 1988 and was never caught. It is possible that, while in the church, he decided to enter upon a program of redemption by voluntarily submerging himself in the baptismal pool, but the evidence suggests that he merely fell through a false ceiling and belly flopped in.

Stephan Lantz, then twenty-seven, was involved in a slight mishap in Hays, Kansas, in 1990. He and Darin Engel, who was driving, were out smashing mailboxes one night, and Engel drove over one that, unknown to him, was mounted on an iron pipe. It caused the truck to become stuck when they drove over it. While Engel shifted between forward and reverse gears to disengage the truck from the mess underneath, Lantz got out to try to pull the mailbox and pipe loose. They were finally successful in freeing the truck, but part of Lantz's thumb remained on the scene. (There was once an actual decapitation incident, in Texas City, Texas, in 1988, attributed to a failed mailbox vandalism caper.)

Everyone driving standard transmission cars lets the clutch slip a little from time to time, but a guy in Miami made perhaps the most expensive slip of all time in 1990. Stopped at a traffic light, he inadvertently let the clutch slip just slightly so that his van drifted backward, just nudging the bumper of the police car behind him. The driver got out to check if damage had occurred, saw that it was a police officer, and took off running in a blaze of speed. Now suspicious, the police impounded the van, obtained a warrant, and found $14 million worth of cocaine inside.

People Who Should Have Considered Holsters

The holster is an important invention, but you wouldn't know it from reading the police blotter. Gunmen often forsake them. Two or three times a year, somewhere in the United States, a guy will be unable to negotiate sticking his gun into his waistband. For all you males, and for all you females who love males, you know what that means: tragedy. Here is just a sampling:

Steven Allen, then twenty-two, of Columbus, Ohio, trying to put his gun into his waistband after robbing the United Dairy Farmers convenience store, shot himself in what was reported as the "groin." Allen later explained yet another gunshot wound, to his foot, by saying that he had accidentally shot himself on a robbery the night before. Stanley Brown, then nineteen, suffered his wound while running off with a woman's purse in Miami, Florida. According to a witness, Brown did not scream when he shot himself (in the groinal area, at least partly specifically within the scrotal area). Rather, he ran a few more steps, stopped, pulled back his waistband to take a look, and exclaimed, "I've been shot!"

Gerald Banks was doing nothing more challenging than standing in a grocery line in Fort Worth, Texas, in 1988, except that he was twirling his gun and fidgeting with the trigger. A shot rang out, and Banks was hit (as police later described it in their report) in "his manhood." Checking out the gun, police discovered it had been stolen, and arrested Banks.

Holsters, men. It's even more important than flossing.

"So I'm A Couple of Days Late With the Rent— What's the Worst That Could Happen to Me?"

Benson Hilt of Evergreen Park, Illinois, made a serious error in 1990 when he forgot to make a rent payment on his safe deposit box at the Standard Bank and Trust Co. Police had been investigating him for drug trafficking; he was fifty-nine years old at the time and in his entire life had reported only $25,000 in income to IRS. As soon as he lost the right to protect the box, the police moved in and tied the contents to drug crimes.

In 1992, a man who had killed his wife and kept her body in a self-storage locker for the last eleven years saw his own world come crashing down. After his wife had been "missing" for a while, he decided to move from the Seattle area, where the locker was located, to Idaho. He had entrusted the monthly locker payments to his new wife. Well, she missed one. The locker company cleaned it out, and Walla Walla has a new resident.

Miscellaneous Poor Decisions

Four teenagers were arrested in the parking lot of the Lakeland (Florida) Square Mall during Christmas season in 1989. They had been trying to break into vehicles in the parking lot and decided on a van with no side windows. They worked on the door for a few seconds, but unfortunately for them, the van was filled with undercover police officers on a stakeout—trying to detect vehicle break-ins during the holiday season. Being kids, these four lacked the experience to be able to detect what might be a stake-out van; certainly, after a few months of sharing cells with professional crooks, they'll pick up enough pointers not to make the same mistake when they get out.

Everton Reed was the guy who really couldn't catch a

break. In 1987, police at the Raleigh-Durham (North Carolina) airport had staked out the luggage carousel, suspecting (courtesy of an informant) that Reed would come to pick up a drug shipment. Upon arriving at the carousel, Reed became suspicious and so passed up his bag. In order to blend in with the other travelers, he casually picked up another piece of luggage and walked away. Police decided to stop him anyway. When they asked him to open the luggage he was carrying, he said he didn't have the key. Police asked if they had his permission to open that suitcase. He said, uh, well, sure. To the great surprise of the police, not to mention Reed, that suitcase happened to contain a bag of marijuana.

Imagine the shock experienced by a five-man gang of robbers who were said to have rushed into a Robert Hall clothing store in Indianapolis and announced a holdup. There was *already* a five-man gang in the store holding it up. One of the ten men happened to fire a shot, causing the other nine to panic. They all grabbed as many clothes off the racks as they could carry, ran for their cars, and raced away. One of the gangs escaped, but Sgt. Harry C. Dunn spotted the other gang and gave chase. The men flung clothing out the window as they tried to escape police, but they were apprehended.

Picking a mugging target is an inexact science, at best. Security consultants suggest ways to advertise that you wouldn't be a good target. Mugger Kim Alberty, then twenty-two, made a bad choice when he accosted a Thai man early one morning in Berkeley, California. An important fact was unknown to Alberty: The man was on his way home from his job as a chef and just happened to be carrying his personal, extensive chef's knife collection. As Alberty began to choke the chef and reach for his wallet, the chef grabbed one of his knives. The news report did not indicate whether Mr. Alberty was diced, sliced, or chopped, but in any event he is no longer with us.

Mickey J. Beard, then eighteen, and two younger companions were arrested in Pleasant Prairie, Wisconsin, in 1991 for trying to steal the wheels off a Chevy Corvette in

a residential garage in the middle of the night. They had three wheels off but suffered a major accident with the fourth when the car fell on one of the thieves. After kicking the car and doing what police called "major damage" to it, the other two then gave up and knocked on the door of the owner's home, asking him to help. The owner flew into a rage and called police, sending the two kids fleeing to their getaway truck. They were found in the truck by police a short time later. They had not been able to drive the truck away because the only one of the three kids who could drive a stick shift was the guy who was trapped under the Corvette.

Sam F. Stewart, then seventeen, was also the victim of a car burglary in the middle of the night. He got into the car, but his problem was his simple inability to disengage the car's electric locks in order to get out. He finally had to use the horn to wake up everyone in the Waskom, Texas, neighborhood in order to draw attention to himself. When police arrived, he was still sitting in the front seat.

People Inattentive to Their Surroundings

Too many criminals to mention here have done themselves in by misdialing a telephone number trying to arrange a drug sale, but reaching a police officer instead. Or they have called their dealer's pager number to reach him just after his arrest. (Police officers are more than happy to return the call and set the trap.) Or they'll just show up at a police station to make a drug dropoff, believing it to be the radio station that was to be the dropoff point because of all the radio antennas outside.

Terry L. Reynolds, then twenty-six, was in traffic court in Hanley Hills, near St. Louis, Missouri, in 1988 and thought he was short $3 to pay his traffic fine. He went outside to the parking lot to ask for the money from his buddy, who didn't have it but did have some marijuana in his car that he could sell to raise the money. (HINT: Terry, the potential client base in the parking lot of a city hall/police department is largely police officers.) Reynolds and his buddy were soon arrested. (In the end,

Reynolds was mistaken; he actually *did* have the $3 on him and need not have engaged in the adventure.)

Aundray Burns, then twenty-six, had an unpromising career halted briefly in 1991 when charged with assault. He came dashing toward some parked cars in New York City, one of them idling with a driver inside. Burns hurriedly opened the door, grabbed the wheel, and tried to displace the driver, yelling frantically, "I gotta go! I gotta go!" Burns was quickly subdued because the driver he tried to displace was New York City transit police officer Daniel Daly—in uniform—and the idling car was an official, well-marked blue and white squad car. Said a spokesman for the Transit Authority police, "What a town, eh?"

"Great Party! Why's Everyone Dressed Like a Cop?"

Theatrical sting operations, by their nature, involve duping not-so-smart criminals. Most of the time, the scams are so well conceived and acted out that even above-average criminals could be forgiven if they fell prey. There is usually a tipoff, though, because, oh, do those fun-loving cops relish leaving clues, mainly for subsequent raconteuring purposes, e.g., "We told them the [fake] wedding was being sponsored by SPOC. Wouldn't one of those guys think to spell that organization backwards? Haw, haw, haw."

There is nothing much here on stings because they're all pretty skillfully done and could trap even smart criminals. This book deals with criminals of above-average stupidity—the cream of doltitude. However, there are a few

people who just don't take to clues so well. These were not *elaborate* stings by police; anybody of only common ignorance could have avoided arrest.

When San Bernardino, California, police closed down a drug factory in a raid in 1987, they had a hard time getting the customers to go away. They even had to flash their badges and threaten to pull their guns to get the customers to leave while they processed the arrests of the dealers. In Huntington Beach, California, in 1991, swarms of police actually had the sellers handcuffed on the ground awaiting the paddy wagon while customers still milled around the scene, *certain* that there must be someone there willing to sell them drugs.

A 1991 prostitution sting in Chattanooga, Tennessee, against johns went forward despite a severe handicap the female decoy was operating under: The vice squad commander, fearing claims of entrapment by those arrested, had told her to wear a hat with the word "POLICE" on it in three-inch letters and to turn so that the customers would be sure to notice the word as they talked to her. Furthermore, the decoy was instructed to admit, if asked, that she was a police officer. Still, three men never noticed, never asked, and were arrested. Sybil Wilson, then twenty, once propositioned an entire truckload of men in Champaign, Illinois, offering them services for a $20-each "group discount," never realizing that they were a police SWAT team.

9

"I Hate It When That Happens":

PEOPLE WHO JUST CAN'T SEEM TO STOP

I remember an old news story that impressed on me the fact that what seems a strong incentive for me might not work on others. A young woman had been arrested for helping her serial-killer boyfriend on his various forays. Technically, she had committed murder in some of the cases, although clearly the boyfriend was the risk to society. The judge felt constrained not to treat her lightly, however, and sentenced her to many years in prison. However, at sentencing, he gave her an out: Because she still had a chance to get her life straight, he would see that she got released to attend the nearby community college, and as long as she made an A or a B, she would stay in school. If she earned a degree, the judge would suspend the rest of the sentence. But if she made a C or below, it was back to the

Big House until she got old and gray. Have you ever heard of a more powerful incentive to make a B? In her first course, she made a C.

Some people are just on that fast-moving freight train to nowhere and cannot seem to get off:

On October 24, 1989, Mr. Kalvin Chambers was released from the Arlington County (Virginia) jail at (according to jail records) 12:03 P.M. According to Arlington police records, he tried to snatch a woman's purse in front of the jailhouse at 12:17 P.M. and was back behind bars before the noon hour was over.

Robert Elliby, then thirty-two, couldn't stop himself, either. Awaiting his trial in a New York City courtroom for theft, he got bored and wandered around. A few minutes later, he was arrested and charged with attempted burglary of a judge's chambers. A young man in Seattle in 1988 was ordered released in Judge Philip Killien's courtroom after having been charged with driving a stolen car. Police say, however, that on his way out of the building, he stopped by the courthouse parking lot and stole a car in order to get home. The car belonged to Killien.

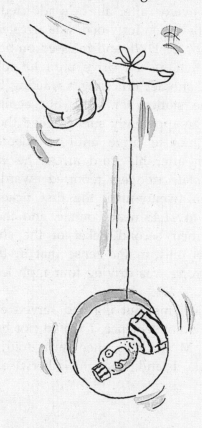

Hilary Parker, then thirty-nine, was arrested in 1991 when he robbed the Citizens Fidelity Bank in Louisville, Kentucky. He had just been released from prison after serving thirteen years for robbing the same bank in 1976. Shawn O'Neill, then forty-two, was back in the slammer in Escondido, California, in 1992 after trying to rob Hussar's Jewelers. He was out on bond at the time, awaiting sentencing for having robbed Hussar's twice three months earlier.

By now, the guy who piles up DWI ticket after DWI ticket is not a novelty; after all, he's addicted. In 1989, John Darcy Bradley, then forty-one, was arrested in Cambridge, Maryland, for DWI, and released on bond under the stipulation that he not drive until he sobered up. Within minutes, another officer was walking Bradley in the door of the station for DWI, but again he was released, when he apparently strengthened the sincerity of his promise not to drive until he sobered up. A short time later, after his third arrest, he was jailed. Two Michigan state troopers reported awarding Bryce Armstrong, then twenty-nine, the first ticket of their shift one night at 11:45 near Pontiac, and then, fifteen minutes later, their second ticket of the shift. (They reported success only in the sense that in the second incident, Armstrong was driving four mph less than in the first.)

Maybe it's just me, but if I had served eighty-nine days of a ninety-day sentence, I would not be thinking escape. Donald M. Thomas, then thirty-four, in jail in Cranston, Rhode Island, thought otherwise. He was captured.

Daniel H. Browning, then thirty-two, just couldn't stop himself, either. He was given a three-day pass from jail in Waukesha, Wisconsin, in order to attend the funeral of his sister. Shortly after his return, it became clear just what form of transportation he had used. He was charged with having stolen cars to get there and back. The second car was found parked across the street from the prison.

People Who Won't Take "No" for an Answer

Two men in Port St. Lucie, Florida, told police in 1990 that Louis Lakes had approached them in Charlie's Bar and tried to sell them drugs. They refused, left, and walked next door to a Subway sandwich shop. Lakes followed them, still touting his drugs. Still, they refused. Finally, Lakes grabbed a knife from the sandwich shop and chased the two men into the parking lot, screaming that he would kill them if they didn't buy drugs. They escaped. Gregory Doster told police he was shot in the head in LaPlace, Louisiana, in 1991 by a drug seller who had arrived just a tad too late to sell him crack cocaine. (Doster had just bought it from another man.) Doster said the man climbed into the passenger seat of Doster's pickup truck and pleaded with him to buy more before shooting him.

Providence, Rhode Island, police lieutenant Richard Tamburini was on his way to a meeting of his undercover team one night when he was flagged down by a prostitute later identified as Patricia Morris. As Tamburini later told a reporter, Morris started to solicit him for sex. He was late for the meeting and did not want to take the time to arrest her, so he tried to help her out by telling her that he thought he saw a police car coming and that she should split. Morris looked all around as Tamburini started to drive away, then lit out after him, yelling, "Hey! There's no police car!" She caught up to him on the next block and continued to shout at him, "There's no cops!"

She chased him for a couple more blocks down the middle of the street, waving at him and cussing—all in an earnest effort to earn her proffered fee of $20—until Tamburini rendezvoused with his team, whereupon Morris was finally arrested.

10

"Bail on That Forgery Charge? Will You Take a Check?":

MISCELLANEOUS BRILLIANT IDEAS

• Twenty-five-year-old Gregory Rosa was arrested as a suspect in a series of vending machine robberies in late 1989 in Portsmouth, Rhode Island, but the only evidence police had on him was that he was loitering around a vending machine one night and then tried, suspiciously, to run away. The police became somewhat more confident of their case, though, when Gregory had the bright idea of paying his own bail at the station. In his knapsack, which he was wearing when arrested, he just happened to have the required $400—in quarters.

• Everyone who is arrested gets one phone call. That's so everyone will have the chance to call a lawyer. Armed robbery suspect Frenchman "Teddy" Glover, then twenty-

one, was accused by police in Wayland, Massachusetts, in 1989, of the additional charge of using his one phone call to threaten the witness who had just reported him. Said the police chief, "I've had prisoners use our telephone to order a pizza, but . . . "

• If lawlessness furnishes average criminoids with a sense of achievement, imagine the satisfaction of *audacious* lawlessness: guys who taunt the police to catch them. Most of the time, cops treat perpetrators like furniture movers treat heavy chests: Take it easy, step by step, don't rush things. Why would criminals *want* to get cops worked up? Answer: Well, it must be because they're stupid. For example, Shelbie Arabie, on the lam in 1988 after a Louisiana prison escape, couldn't resist sending cops a series of "having a swell time—catch me if you can" postcards. He was captured in Tavernier, Florida, in a routine traffic check. The guards back at Angola were just delighted to see him.

• Antwan Robinson and his brother had the bright idea of kidnapping a drug dealer for ransom. That's a daunting and risky task for even the most experienced criminals, but the brothers Robinson were just eighteen and sixteen, respectively. They waited outside what they thought was the man's house and grabbed an arriving occupant of a car, who turned out to be an eighteen-year-old woman. After exchanging gunfire with a man inside, they drove off with the woman in her car and later called to demand $18,000 ransom from her family. When the family balked, the brothers concluded that they must have staked out the wrong house. After much bickering between themselves, they finally abandoned the scheme and released the woman, who drove home in her car, which was by this time loaded with the Robinsons' fingerprints. Their principal reason for abandoning the project: Antwan had to be home by 10 P.M. because that's when the electronic monitoring device on his ankle kicked in. He was forced to wear it as a condition of his release on an earlier criminal charge.

• At least the Robinsons had the sense to abandon a bad idea. In Baton Rouge, Louisiana, in 1991, Daniel Smith and Louis Reed, both twenty-seven at the time, needed a car and were partial to a big green Impala, which they drove away, without the courtesy of notifying the owner. Soon, many people in the vicinity were admiring the car, including several police officers. The main reason is that the car was being driven backward, at speeds estimated at around thirty mph, on a fairly busy thoroughfare, as the pair searched for a gas station. They had stolen a car with no forward gears, but it did not occur to them to get out of the car and find another one.

• You can't really blame Robert Hernandez for wanting to appeal his sixty-five-year prison sentence, which he received in 1987 in a murder trial in Dallas. He fought for, and was granted, a new trial in 1988, saying that he was unfairly treated when prosecutors told the jurors that they shouldn't worry about the length of Hernandez's sentence because he might be let out early on parole. That was clearly an error, said an appeals court, and another trial was held. The new jury gave him ninety years.

• Juan Mas, at the time (1985) sales manager of Action Auto Brokers in Opa-Locka, Florida, thought he'd branch out into drugs. He set up a deal intending to rip some buyers off. That he was still a sales manager at heart was clear from the fact that when the buyers mused that they'd like to buy a Ford Escort, Mas gave them his card. Later, the card was found on one of the buyers after Mas had nearly killed him. (Mas *did* kill the other.)

•It's a well-known tactic of apartment-house living that when planning a loud party, you always invite the neighbors so as to reduce the chances that they'll report your ruckus to the police. Billy Dale Anderson, then twenty-two, and David Cabarett, then thirty-three, should have been so wily. They tried to break out of Okanogan County Jail in Washington by chipping through a concrete wall eight inches thick. The piece of metal they were using made so much noise for so long that several inmates complained to guards, and the men were apprehended. (If the two *had* chipped through the concrete, they would have found themselves on a landing eighty feet above the ground.)

Their Own Worst Critics

Substantial research indicates that criminals are perfectionists of sorts. They believe in their ability—once they commit to it—to make a scam work and to escape undetected. Nowhere does this failed perfectionism show up more starkly than when the probable small-time felon (or, even better, a probable misdemeanant) becomes so dissatisfied with his work that he decides to check out of life early. Try these hasty, yet ultimate, sacrifices:

Mailman Charles Palmer departed us two days before his trial for mail fraud in Hilton Head, South Carolina. His troubles started a couple of years before, when he had become dissatisfied with an optometrist's misprescribing his eyeglasses. Palmer then allegedly ordered more than three hundred magazine subscriptions for the eye doctor (bill me later,

of course). Oh, the shame of public accusation for *that!* Jeez, Charles, wouldn't it have been easier just to see if F. Lee Bailey were available? Ditto Texan Danny Ray Davis, who checked out the night before he was scheduled to testify before a grand jury investigating cheating in a series of professional bass-fishing tournaments. A shotgun blast to the head seemed preferable to the certain ignominy in store for him.

Profit and Loss Statements

To be judged successful, money-type crime should yield a sufficient return on the investment of risk—risk of the arrest record, fine or jail time, and/or potential death at the hands of overzealous cops or resisting victims. While individual criminals set their own preferences in the ratio of reward to risk, I'm pretty sure that some crimes must be regarded as failures by any standards.

A never-apprehended fella knocked at the door of the unritzy home of a Dallas man, gained entry with a gun, and began rummaging through the house while holding the owner at bay. After a quick tour, he concluded that there was no jewelry or other portable valuables and asked the owner for money. Emptying the wallet produced $8. Dejected, but determined to move on, the robber took the money and proceeded to the door, but then abruptly stopped, turned around, flung the $8 back, and declared, "This house is not worth robbing." The torture of mixed emotions hits hard: What homeowner wants to hear that?

Thomas J. Schooley, then twenty, was arrested for an alley robbery of two men in Evansville, Indiana, in 1990. The men emptied their pockets, but Schooley came away with only eleven cents. (HINT: Thomas, rich people don't hang out in alleys at night. Most people in alleys at night are probably just other criminals.)

Other such robberies I've heard about involved booty consisting of a cigarette and a small box of Popsicles (which actually helped police locate the thieves when they came upon a car with two men inside and a bunch of Popsicle sticks on the ground).

One scenario that is extremely unflattering to members of the robbery community is popping up more and more recently. I first saw it in the crime column of the *Wichita* (Kansas) *Eagle* of April 11, 1990. A man walked into a gas station and laid $2 on the counter, asking for a pack of cigarettes. It was all a diversion, however. When the clerk turned to fetch the cigarettes and ring up the sale, the customer reached into the cash drawer, grabbed all the paper he could see, and ran out the door. However, the clerk said later, he had just bundled the cash and put it into the in-store drop, so that, to the best of his recollection, the paper contents of the cash drawer consisted of several pieces of paper and a single dollar bill. The robber, of course, had left the original $2 on the counter, giving himself a negative cash flow.

But the epitome of haplessness has to be the guy who broke into the Towles Coffee Shop in Burlingame, California, in 1992. He forced open a window to get in, then tried to open a safe and a metal cabinet, but found both locked. Apparently frustrated and not willing to leave empty-handed, he saw a "penny cup" beside the cash register and swiped approximately thirty cents in change.

11

"The Bank Is Loaded on Friday—It's Payday for Cops":

PEOPLE IN THE WRONG PLACE AT THE WRONG TIME

You only have to walk around to know that some people have a malfunctioning sixth sense that tells them, foolishly, to do *this*, be *there*, try *that*. These are the people who just can't get it right—the "20" in the old 80–20 principle: 80 percent of the world's screwups happen to 20 percent of the people. (Actually, it seems to me more a 96-4 principle.) These guys just can't catch a break:

Jesus Henderson, then twenty-two, was arrested in St. Paul, Minnesota, while fleeing the sandwich shop he had just robbed. His escape route happened to take him past a police precinct station during a shift change, as many officers were going in and out of the building. Or take William

Whitaker, then twenty-seven, who was arrested after a shootout in an AmeriFirst Bank in Miami, Florida, in 1989. He had marched in, gun drawn and head covered in stocking cap—while an FBI agent was in the bank showing a suspect's picture to get information on a robbery of the same bank two weeks earlier. (The suspect in the earlier robbery was, of course, Whitaker himself.)

The least fortunate escapee I've heard about is Michael Michell, who went over the wall in Montana in 1991 and *did* get out of the state. He hid out in Washington, and one night decided to attend a Seattle Mariners baseball game. He was in line at a souvenir stand at the ballpark, but right in front of him happened to be Montana State Prison warden Jack McCormick, who was attending the baseball game while on vacation. McCormick later said, "He was real surprised to see me. I said, 'Hi, Mike, how are you doing?'"

No story is more pathetic than that of Darnell Madison—make that the *late* Darnell Madison. He had spotted a guy with a wad of money hanging around Homewood, Alabama, and had shadowed him to a motel room. He drew his gun and rushed the room, intending to deprive the man of the cash. Turns out the man with the money was one of seven undercover police officers working on a drug case. There they all were, heavily armed, and Darnell barely knew what hit him.

Police in Arlington, Texas, were greatly assisted in solving a 1991 armored car robbery. The robber, with gun in hand running for his car, just happened to have parked beside a busload of Japanese tourists, who aimed their cameras when they heard the commotion. Many prints of the man's face and license plate became available, and he was picked up a short time later.

Just Won't Leave Well Enough Alone

In a special category are criminals who get away with one crime, and thus could be going along their merry way, yet who just can't resist calling attention to themselves in some way that proves to be their undoing.

Kharl Fulton of Louisville, Kentucky, was hiding out in Los Angeles on drug charges but then decided to apply to become a contestant on the TV show "The Price Is Right." He was spotted on the tube by a former co-worker in Louisville, who notified authorities, who searched the biographical information Fulton filled out for the show's producers. Contributing to the ease of the co-worker's identification was Fulton's decision to use his real name, including the oddly spelled "Kharl."

Rick Bosco, then thirty-six, had the misfortune to be standing at the cash register of a Park Ridge, Illinois, hardware store, poised to write one more in a series of bad checks, when who should capture the clerk's attention but police officers. They had come into the store to show employees an artist's sketch of the man wanted for passing bad checks. Bosco excused himself, but police apprehended him soon after.

Amanda Guild ran from drug charges in Jackson, Tennessee, all the way to Saginaw, Michigan. She joined a bowling league there, rolling an uneventful average of 131. But she had one series, in October 1990, when she was "in' the zone," rolling 587 for three games. She was named "Bowler of the Week," and her photo appeared in the local paper. The photo was spotted by an IRS agent familiar with the Tennessee case, and she was arrested at her team's next practice.

12

"I Didn't Do It, and Furthermore, I Didn't Mean To":

JUDGMENT DAYS

Eventually, incompetent criminals tend to end up in court. There at last, one would think, they would be protected from themselves. The Constitution purposely makes it very difficult for people to screw themselves in court. Formal rules of procedure and evidence, layers of appeals courts, and hyperactive defense lawyers examining every nuance of a trial conspire to create a facade of innocence for even the lowest riffraff. Still, some crimino-Americans (who, because of the presumption of innocence, should better be labeled accuso-Americans) defeat even these near-foolproof safeguards.

Silence, especially for criminals, is golden. In 1985, veteran defendant Dennis Newton was on trial for armed robbery in an Oklahoma City courtroom. He had a court-appointed lawyer beside him, but according to the assistant district attorney, Newton was notorious around the courthouse for grilling witnesses himself. This time, the alleged victim, a gas station clerk, was testifying and happened to point a finger at Newton identifying him as the one who robbed her. (HINT: Dennis, you had a lawyer. Let her ask the questions. That's why she's there.) Newton then jumped up, calling the clerk a liar, adding, "I should have blown your fucking head off ... [revelatory pause; light bulb goes on] ... if I'd been the one that was there."

Jeffrey Johnson made a similarly bad judgment in trying to defend himself against a charge of robbing a Texaco station in Wilmington, Delaware. Johnson maintained that he was somewhere else at the time. A police officer was testifying about the crime scene and referred to the female clerk-victim not as the victim but as a witness. (In fact, she was the *only* witness to the crime.) Johnson leaped to his feet and blurted out, "What are you talking about, some 'witness,' man? There was only me and her in the store."

"Dennis, Be Sure to Wear Your Drug Possession *Uniform* to Your Drug Possession Trial"

The idea of a crime persona initially struck me when I met the first criminal defendant I ever represented in court. I went downstairs to the basement lockup at the District of Columbia Superior Court and called out "Tony McKinley" to the cellfull of arrestees. None of the twenty-five or so men moved, including the one sitting on the table directly in front of me. I called five more times, in an increasingly louder voice. Nothing. After a pause of ten seconds, the gent on the table suddenly sprang to life. "Oh, right here, man." I stared at him, fearing that anyone who missed my hollering of his name had to be on drugs, which would hurt him in his imminent courtroom appearance that might or might not result in his pretrial release. "No, man, I'm not on drugs. I just didn't hear you." Huh? "Tony McKinley, man. That's not my real name. That's just my crime name."

What did in Christopher Plovie was his crime *uniform*.

117

He was on trial in Pontiac, Michigan, contesting his arrest for cocaine possession, claiming that the police search of him was unconstitutional because his jacket did not "bulge up." A police officer had testified that he was entitled to search Plovie's jacket pocket because there was a bulge, which could have been a weapon that could have been used against the officer. Plovie in fact had worn to court the same jacket he had been wearing when arrested. His lawyer insisted that the judge look at the jacket to see that it would not bulge up. Plovie handed him the jacket. The judge examined it, then put his hand inside the pocket that was supposed to have bulged up. He found a *new* packet of cocaine. Since Plovie had handed over the jacket willingly, no claim of unconstitional search could stand up this time, but the judge accepted a guilty plea to the other charge instead.

"I Coulda Beat the Rap":
Screwing Up the Plea Bargain

To save time and expense, in virtually every criminal case in the country, the prosecutor offers the defendant a plea bargain—sometimes a great deal, sometimes only a modest improvement over a straight admission of the charges. The idea is to make going to trial such a risk for the defendant that he will plead guilty to fewer or lesser charges. The defendant's lawyer operates as a governor of the defendant's decision, preventing the defendant from making truly bad judgments, but lawyers can't stop everything. For better or worse, defendants almost always take plea bargains. For one thing, they give the defendant something to talk about while he's in the Big House: Sure, I'm innocent, man, they didn't have no evidence, man, but it was my *lawyer*, man, *he* made me take that plea bargain.

The saddest sacks are those who reject the plea bargain all the way through trial but then get cold feet right around the time the jury starts deliberating. A sharp prosecutor who fears that the government has lost the case can sometimes reoffer the plea bargain agreement and take advantage of the defendant's anxiety.

Russell Barnes is but one example of the thesis. He got three and a half years in St. Paul, Minnesota, for aggravated larceny in 1990. The jury had been deliberating for eight hours, into the night, on six counts. Barnes, increasingly scared of a conviction, pleaded guilty to one count in exchange for dropping the other five—at the same time that the jurors were at last formalizing their verdict of *not* guilty on all counts. The plea stood. Said Barnes's lawyer when the verdict was read in court, "It was like O. Henry meets Alfred Hitchcock." He said that Barnes "went into shock, and so did his lawyer." One juror, who did not know about Barnes's guilty plea, saw a tear in Barnes's eye at the reading of the verdict and walked over to congratulate him. (After Barnes had served almost two years of the sentence, the Minnesota Court of Appeals overturned his sentence.)

Dissing the Judge

Few human beings hold as much power over a person as a judge does at sentencing. In a "two-ta-ten" sentence, there's a big difference between two and ten. There's even more difference between having to serve a sentence and hearing those magic words "probation" or "suspended sentence." Nonetheless, many defendants are not on their best behavior when they stand before the judge at sentencing.

Some people charged with DWI show up in the middle of a bender. An Encino, California, school bus driver, Harold Keith Lone, then forty and recently convicted of drunken driving charges, stumbled into court one morning in 1990 to be sentenced. He was reeking of alcohol, shouting obscenities in the hallway, mumbling to the judge, but insisting he wasn't impaired. "No way," he said. "No way, Jose."

Bad enough that welfare caseworker Rosemarie Leitzell, then fifty-two, was convicted of embezzling over $260,000 from the local government in Martinsville, Indiana. As she stood before the judge for sentencing, she thought it would help her request for probation if she handed the judge this poem:

So you've heard it all, judge.
I'm not slime and not sludge;
Just a person who went the wrong way.
As I stand before you with friends,
It is true that I'm living the worst of my fears.
But perhaps you agree,
With these friends here with me,
That I shouldn't be sent up for years.

The judge didn't say what he had planned to give her before he heard the poem, but after he heard it, she got fourteen years. (HINT: Rosemarie, there is *nothing* worse. Better pedophilia than bad poetry.)

Actually, the best stories of courtroom idiocy were ones I wasn't able to verify and which might have had the fragrance of "urban legends." These stories might have come only from cops and lawyers sitting around a bar at night, embellishing only modestly funny stories. Still, they could be true.

Such as, for instance, the lawyer's asking the witness to identify the people he saw rob him. If all goes well, the witness will point to the three men sitting at the defense table. Question: "Are the men who robbed you in the courtroom today?" Answer: "Yes." Question: "Where are they?" Before the witness can give an answer, the three defendants raise their hands.

Another possible urban legend occurred in the setting of a police interrogation. Carrying a Radnor, Pennsylvania, dateline on the UPI wire in the mid-eighties was the story of Judge Ira Garb's tossing out charges against a hapless defendant who fell for too ridiculous an interrogation

method. The suspect was not familiar with lie detectors but was apparently willing to take a test. Detectives placed a metal colander on his head with wires running to a nearby Xerox machine. On the Xerox machine's glass copy plate was a sheet of paper with the words, "HE'S LYING." When the suspect made a statement, a detective pushed a button ("PRINT) on the Xerox machine, delivering a copy of the sheet of paper, which was then shown to the suspect. After a while, he confessed.

However, a couple of these kinds of stories apparently really happened. One created a real test for the Texas Court of Appeals on whether the defendant got a fair trial. Billy Ray Ford was on the stand testifying that he was innocent of the robberies he was charged with, and after a while, the judge took a brief recess. When Ford resumed testifying, the judge asked him whether, during the recess, he had talked to any of the witnesses outside the courtroom. (He wasn't supposed to.) Why, yes, said Ford (again under oath), as a matter of fact I did. Which ones, asked the judge. Answered Ford, "The ones that I robbed." The Court of Appeals turned down Ford's appeal.

And Dereese Delon Waddell, then twenty-seven, was charged in St. Louis Park, Minnesota, with purse-snatching after he failed elementary smarts in a police lineup. The seventy-six-year-old victim was asked to pick out her assailant, and Waddell was ushered into the lineup room. Police told Waddell to fix the bill of his cap to conform with how the woman remembered her assailant wearing it. According to police officers, Waddell protested the instruction, saying, "No, put it on [me] backwards. That's the way I had it on when I took the purse."

13

"And the Award for Outstanding Stupidity Goes To . . . ":

AMERICA'S LEAST COMPETENT CRIMINALS

Almost all of you will ask yourselves, "Well, Chuck, *all* these guys are stupid, but which one is *the stupidest?*" Which one has pushed the envelope the most? There is much competition.

It could be David Posman, then thirty-three, who had actually devoted some time to planning his armored-truck robbery in Providence, Rhode Island. For example, he had a disguise to assist his getaway—elaborate and frilly women's clothing. However, things did not proceed as planned. He held up the truck while it was stopped in downtown Providence and forced the driver to cruise to the next block, which he had remembered in planning as relatively unpopulated. Not that day. That day, it was a construction site crowded with workers. Undeterred, but with a dozen workers looking on, he grabbed four bags of money, hurriedly changed into his disguise, and very slowly lugged the heavy sacks, heading toward his truck, which he had parked in an alley a block away. One of the construction workers followed the female-appearing, bag-toting Posman until he glimpsed a meter maid on the street and told her to call the police. Within minutes, the police had arrested Posman. In the meantime, he had driven the wrong way in the alley and had angered a delivery driver, who was evidently not impressed with Posman's sexy outfit—especially the three-day growth of beard. The four bags Posman had chosen to carry away contained nothing but pennies, for a total heist of around $200. Posman's planning failed on another score as well: his female wardrobe was incomplete below the waist. He had brought sheer black lacy pantyhose but nothing to wear over them.

It could be the guy with two guns who tried to hold up Houston, Texas, convenience store clerk Wazir Jiwi in 1990. Jiwi told police that he got to talking with the man and eventually offered him money for each of the guns in succession until he had closed the deal and had both in his possession. During the negotiations, Jiwi had pushed a button automatically locking the front door so that after he had handed over the $200 for the two guns, he made the robber give back the money in order to be let out the door.

Dumbest? It could be Ronald McClanahan. McClanahan, then forty-one, was arrested in Columbia, Missouri, in 1989. His first mistake was to try to knock off a gun shop while armed only with a knife. At first, he had the drop on the clerks and held them at bay while he tried to open the electronic cash register—despite his not having the slightest clue as to how to do that. He randomly pushed buttons for a minute or so, becoming increasingly frustrated. Then he decided to pick up the whole thing and carry it away, but of course it was plugged into the wall, and when he had taken a few quick steps, he lost control of the register, as it stayed attached to the wall while he kept walking. Both he and the cash register fell to the floor, which enabled a store clerk to grab a gun and move in on McClanahan. At first, said store employees, McClanahan lay perfectly still on the floor as the gun was pointed at him. Then McClanahan yelled, "Go ahead and shoot me," scrambled to his feet, grabbed the register again, and started for the door. The clerk held his fire. The register again fell from his hands, and this time the drawer came loose, sending money all over the floor. McClanahan reached down, grabbed as many bills as he could, and ran for the exit; but by that time enough employees had gathered to block the door and grab him. Even though he could not escape before police arrived, McClanahan refused to loosen his grip on the money, and police had to use force to pry it from his hands.

It could be Dwight Harold Riser, then thirty-eight, who wasn't sure whether he wanted to live or die when he took two maids hostage at the Economy Inn in Ruston, Louisiana, in 1987 and held them for eight hours, frequently exchanging gunfire with police. The standoff ended only after Riser decided that his salvation lay in achieving holy matrimony with one of the maids. He called for a minister, who performed a wedding ceremony by telephone (but the minister had his fingers crossed at the time, so it didn't count), after which Riser surrendered.

Child-support miscreant James Graham was treated kindly by Judge Jerry Leonard in Raleigh, North Carolina, in 1988: Graham would not be sent to jail, said Leonard, if he would merely write ten thousand times, "I must pay my child support on time" and give the paperwork to the judge. Graham handed in his assignment but soon fell further behind in the payments, causing Leonard to take a closer look at Graham's homework. He found that line number "10,000" displayed a proud star of achievement from Graham, but he also found that the submission was done in at least three different styles of handwriting and that the 1,015th line was followed immediately by the 2,089th line. In fact, there were only 2,192 lines in the 10,000-line document. Graham was immediately jailed.

The story of Michael Anderson Goodwin is full of irony and sadness. He spent time on South Carolina's death row in the early eighties for murder, but his appeal of the death sentence was successful, and his date with destiny was changed to life in prison. In 1988, while sitting naked on a metal toilet in his prison cell and attempting to repair his small television set by biting into a wire to trim it, he was electrocuted.

It could be a guy named Morgan, as in State v. Morgan, a 1991 Arkansas prosecution of a sixty-three-year-old man for rape. He had perhaps heard about one of the handful of cases in the U.S. in which a rape defendant is allowed to show—always via photographs—that his penis is physically inconsistent with the description offered by the victim. Typically, victim says circumcised, defendant shows uncircumcised. Or victim says small, defendant shows huge. Mr. Morgan at trial exposed to the jury, without benefit of photograph, his *unerect* penis, for the purpose, he said, of proving that he could not obtain the erection necessary to have committed rape. "See there?" one can imagine him saying gleefully to the jurors. Mr. Morgan is now a permanent resident of the Big House.

Tajiwder Brar, twenty-seven, committed one of the least explicable series of property crimes in 1989, when he tried to vent his wrath over the disappointing sales of his new book, *The Emotional Generator*. (Brar was a graduate student in nuclear engineering at the University of Cincinnati; his book was a philosophical work on "achieving success through materialism.") He had placed ads for the book in the campus newspaper, but the ads were deficient in that nowhere did the ads mention how anyone could obtain the book—stores, phone number, mailing address. Further, Brar apparently wrote his own ad copy, limited to this line: "In the USA, in the East, about the philosophy of your life on this planet only." Not surprisingly, the ad generated no sales. Brar was arrested for setting fires, in retaliation, to seven campus newspaper boxes that contained copies of the newspaper.

Or how about Vincent Federico. Organized-crime figures have reputations for toughness, but not necessarily cleverness. Following a 1989 contract killing, rival families started consolidating. One side, the Patriarca family, planned a major new-member initiation ceremony. The FBI knew about the meeting but did not know where it would take place. Vincent Federico was an important participant, except for one thing: He was still in jail. However, he had applied for a furlough the weekend of October 29, 1989 (you know the tradition of Massachusetts prison furloughs), and had listed his sister's house in Medford, Massachusetts, as his destination. The FBI put two and two together and bugged the house, coming down with massive amounts of evidence against Raymond Patriarca and others.

When picking out the dumbest, it may not be fair to include drunk drivers. By definition, they don't know what

they're doing. However, occasionally they act so preposter-
ously stupid, brilliantly stupid, even, that observers must
question the premises under which they operate when they
are sober.

Take the guy in Marshfield, Wisconsin, in 1981, who was
sitting in his van parked alongside the road as Deputy Sheriff
Mark Gosh was making his rounds. The guy was draped
over the steering wheel with the doors locked. Pounding on
the door did not wake the man, so Gosh started rocking the
vehicle. Suddenly the "driver" sat bolt upright from his deep
sleep and grabbed the steering wheel for dear life, nervously
making driving motions. Finally Gosh got his attention, and
the man rolled down the window. "How fast were you
going?" asked Gosh. Without a blink, the man said, "Fifty-
five."

But, with all due respect, my choice is Bruce Damon. In
1987, he held up the Mutual Federal Savings Bank in the
Hanover Mall near Brockton, Massachusetts. He produced a
gun and demanded that the teller free up "$40 million" for
him. The teller informed him that the bank only keeps about
$40,000 on the premises. Okay, said Damon, forty million,
forty thousand, fine. Damon then hit him with this stunner:
He didn't want cash; he wanted a *check*. He was arrested a
short time later when he tried to deposit the check into his
account at another bank. Sentence: three to five years. Cut to
July 1991, Mutual Federal Savings Bank in Halifax, Massachusetts. Taking cash this time, he made off with $43,000
but was apprehended at a roadblock nearby. Cut to his sentencing hearing, February 1992, Brockton Superior Court.
The prosecutor is demanding a sentence of eight-to-fifteen.
"Incredible!" countered Damon. After all, he said, he only

got three-to-five last time. The judge replied matter-of-factly, "You can expect the time to go up each time you rob a bank." Second argument for Damon: "[E]very cent of the money was recovered when I was apprehended." Third argument: "I don't even think I put [the bank employees] in fear. The whole [robbery] was extremely passive." Fourth argument: He reached into his pocket and pulled out a newspaper story indicating that the bank's earnings actually rose in the time period following the robbery. "I didn't hurt this bank at all," he said. Finally, exasperated, the judge wondered out loud, "If you were out today, would you do it again, Mr. Damon?" Damon replied, "I'd like to plead the Fifth Amendment on that." The judge could only do what you and I have been doing throughout this book: shake our heads in amazement.

SOURCES

The Ann Arbor News
The Argus (Fremont, California)
The Argus (Rock Island, Illinois)
Arkansas Court Bulletin
The Arlington Journal (Arlington, Virginia)
Associated Press
Austin American-Statesman (Austin, Texas)
Barberton Herald (Barberton, Ohio)
The Boston Globe
Hillsborough/Burlingame Boutique Villager (Burlingame,
    California)
Cavalier Daily (Charlottesville, Virginia)
Central West End Journal (suburban St. Louis, Missouri)
Chattanooga News–Free Press
Chicago Tribune
Columbia Daily Tribune (Columbia, Missouri)
The Columbus Dispatch (Columbus, Ohio)
The Commercial Appeal (Memphis, Tennessee)
The Courier–Journal (Louisville, Kentucky)

Daily News (Los Angeles)
Daily Texan (Austin)
The Daily Times (Pryor, Oklahoma)
Democrat and Chronicle (Rochester, New York)
The Des Moines Register
Detroit Free Press
The Duluth News-Tribune (Duluth, Minnesota)
Eagle Times (Reading, Pennsylvania)
Editor & Publisher
The Edmonton Journal (Edmonton, Alberta)
The El Paso Times
The Enterprise (Brockton, Massachusetts)
The Free Press (Mankato, Minnesota)
Gainesville Sun (Gainesville, Florida)
Greensboro News & Record
Houston Chronicle
The Houston Post
The Human Ecologist
The Hutchinson News (Hutchinson, Kansas)
The Indianapolis News
The Indianapolis Star
Journal and Constitution (Atlanta)
The Journal-Bulletin (Providence, Rhode Island)
The Kansas City Star
The Knoxville Journal
Lenexa Sun (Overland Park, Kansas)
Los Angeles Times
The Miami Herald
Nashville Banner
The National Law Journal
The New Rochelle Standard-Star (New Rochelle, New York)

The New York Times
New York Post
The Palm Beach Post (West Palm Beach, Florida)
Patriot-News (Harrisburg, Pennsylvania)
The Philadelphia Inquirer
Portland Press-Herald (Portland, Maine)
Rochester Post-Bulletin (Rochester, Minnesota)
Rocky Mountain News (Denver)
The Salt Lake Tribune
The San Diego Union
San Francisco Chronicle
San Francisco Examiner
San Jose Mercury-News
The SandPaper (Ocean County, New Jersey)
Santa Barbara News-Press
The Sault Star (Sault Ste. Marie, Ontario)
Seattle Post-Intelligencer
Southeast Missourian (Cape Girardeau, Missouri)
Sports Illustrated
St. Louis Post-Dispatch
St. Louis Park Sun-Sailor (St. Louis Park, Minnesota)
The Star-Ledger (Newark, New Jersey)
Star-News (Pasadena, California)
Star Tribune (Minneapolis)
The Sun (Baltimore)
Sun-Sentinel (Ft. Lauderdale, Florida)
Sun-Times (Chicago)
The Tennessean (Nashville)
United Press International
USA Today
The Washington Post
The Washington Times

Watertown Public Opinion (Watertown, South Dakota)
White Plains Reporter Dispatch (White Plains, New
    York)
The Wichita Eagle
Wisconsin State Journal (Madison)

ABOUT THE AUTHOR

Chuck Shepherd compiles the weekly "News of the Weird" column that appears in about two hundred daily and weekly newspapers in the United States and Canada (distributed by Universal Press Syndicate). He is co-author (with John J. Kohut and Roland Sweet) of the paperback books *News of the Weird* (1989), *More News of the Weird* (1990), and *Beyond News of the Weird* (1991). He has collected weird news since the late seventies and began writing "News of the Weird" in 1988.

Shepherd was formerly a lawyer for the federal government (Federal Communications Commission, Federal Trade Commission), a criminal defense attorney in Washington, D.C., and a professor at the business school of George Washington University.